IN AND OUT OF COURT

Nigel Thomson

IN AND OUT OF COURT

The legal life and musical times
of
Sheriff Nigel Thomson

DUNEDIN ACADEMIC PRESS
EDINBURGH

Published by
Dunedin Academic Press
8 Albany Street
Edinburgh EH1 3QB

ISBN 1 903765 03 X

British Library Cataloguing in Publication Data

A catalogue record for this book is available from
the British Library

Typeset by Trinity Typing
Printed in Great Britain by Polestar, Aberdeen

Dedication

To Lolo

Contents

Acknowledgements

I acknowledge with many thanks the tremendous amount of work done on the text by my daughter Ingalo. A rigorously professional freelance editor, she was not a bit reluctant to point out to me my errors, stylistic and otherwise. I also gratefully acknowledge the assistance given to me by my neighbour and computer consultant Henry Wilson, who answered many SOS calls to my word processor.

Above all I would like to thank my wife Lolo for her encouragement to me in writing these memoirs. She has so enhanced all aspects of my life, and has in particular relieved the care and burden of my law with the joy and delight of her music.

I should add that my essay on sentencing (Appendix One) originally appeared in the *Scots Law Times*, and the 'whipping' part of the chapter on Peebles Sheriff Court was featured in the *Journal of the Law Society of Scotland*. Finally, the tunes for the original songs quoted in the text may be obtained from me on request.

Nigel Thomson

Foreword

by

The Hon. Lord Davidson

It is an honour to be invited to write a foreword for the memoirs of Nigel Thomson. We first met in Edinburgh at a family wedding in 1951. Half a century later I have my own recollections of one who played a leading part in the legal and artistic life of Scotland during that period. In and out of court Nigel displayed originality and excellent judgment in the worlds of the Law and of Music. Although he lost both parents when he was very young, his early life was happy and, after he met Lolo, truly romantic. For him and Lolo much of the joy of living happily ever after has come from the dedication of their outstanding gifts in equal measure to the Law and Music.

In this book Nigel immediately dispels any suspicion that the reader may have about memoirs written by one whose life has been spent in the Law. Is the subject matter too trivial and remote in time to merit attention? Does the author have an agenda of his own, with self-justification as its driving force? Does he have old scores to pay off? These questions invite an affirmative answer in too many legal autobiographies. It is therefore a pleasure to report that in Nigel's memoirs all these familiar questions are answered with a resounding 'No'.

In his treatment of the legal world Nigel is cool and detached. In spite of his having served as a Sheriff for over thirty years, he firmly curbs the temptation to recount nothing but anecdotes culled from cases in which he had at one time been involved. Instead, he takes a global view of the courts, making shrewd criticisms of the Court of Session as it was when he passed advocate in 1953. At that time it was generally reckoned that no one in practice at the Bar starved, but part of the price of the advantage lay in the drudgery of handling work which for the most part was dull and monotonous.

When the time came to decide whether or not to take silk, Nigel preferred the shrieval bench. The reason which he gives for that decision is a curious one. He ruled himself out as an applicant for silk on the ground that he lacked sufficeint self-confidence. One consequence of this lack was that he found himself being too readily persuaded of the superiority of the arguments advanced by the other side. Although it is hard to accept that Nigel suffered from lack of self-confidence, that was his belief, and there is no reason to suppose that he ever had cause to regret his decision.

As a Sheriff Nigel brought an original, and highly personal, approach to the conduct of court business. In his early years he was frustrated by the limited range of disposals open to the court in criminal cases. His account of the occasions when he persuaded guilty persons to write an essay about themselves deserves close attention. Whatever the reader may think about the merits of that innovation, the narrative reveals the determination of a humane judge to do all in his power to quicken the pace of penal reform.

Nigel outlines the events that culminated in the development of the Town Mill Theatre in Strathaven, where he and his family lived while he was a Sheriff at Hamilton. In a city a project like the Strathaven Town Mill would be more likely to encounter indifference than outright hostility. But for long it has been notorious that in towns like Strathaven 'incomers' require to display rare qualities of personality and boundless patience before they can confidently regard themselves as having been accepted by the local community. It is a striking tribute to Nigel's personal qualities that so many showed their confidence in his leadership by giving generously of their time, skill and money to bring the Arts to Strathaven.

Any reader who was present at the original performances will respond with pleasure to the songs with which Nigel used to delight audiences at Bar dinners and other social functions. To many of the lyrics which were sung at these performances Nigel contributed words and music, giving some of them a sharp, but measured, satirical edge directed at the legal establishment.

Throughout his career Nigel enjoyed an unsurpassed reputation as an entertainer. This truth is borne out by editors of the Stair Memorial Encyclopedia who invited him to write the article entitled 'Entertainment'. The opening sentence of that title is in the following terms:- 'The British are said to take their pleasures sadly; and in so far as they take their pleasures in Scotland, the law does little to reduce the sadness.' Passages of that quality are hard to find in the Encyclopedia, and they must have come as 'balm in Gilead' to the editors when they turned their attention to that title after wrestling with the arid complexities of tax and employment law. I venture to suggest, however, that the sentence quoted above requires amendment. That is because, thanks to Nigel, Lolo and their friends, Scots of today have learned to enjoy their musical pleasures in a mood of sheer delight.

C. K. Davidson

Starting Out

Son of the manse

My father was a minister. My maternal grandfather was a
minister. So was my maternal great-grandfather. So too was my
maternal great-great-grandfather. I count myself very privileged
to have had a manse upbringing in the 1930s. There were great
benefits – you lived in a continual atmosphere of loving-
kindness, you experienced daily family prayer and bible-reading,
you met all sorts of people, and you found you had an immediate
affinity with other sons and daughters of the manse. But there
were also considerable drawbacks – there was never any money
for the holidays abroad and so many other activities which are
commonplace today for youngsters, and it was a very inward-
looking world you lived in. I was only aware of life in the church,
and had no idea of adult social life, no idea of the business world,
no idea of political life. As far as I knew, the world ended at the
boundaries of the Edinburgh Presbytery.

My father was greatly beloved as a pastor by his congregation
of Mayfield North, Edinburgh, and, being a frequent broadcaster,
was greatly admired as a preacher throughout Scotland. When
one member heard of my father's sudden death in 1939 he said,
'I felt as if I didn't have a friend left in the world.' I was aged only
twelve when he died, and as my mother had died when I was
barely three, I never had the experience of family life in a normal
married household, and I particularly regretted not having had
my father to guide me in the spiritual life. But my involvement
in manse life continued, since the wonderful lady we called
'Aunt Lucy' who came to look after me and my two elder
brothers on our mother's death (and who continued to look
after me until her own death three weeks before my marriage

thirty-five years later) was herself a daughter of the manse. When my father died, she and I moved to live with my maternal grandfather who was Dr R.J. Drummond, the senior minister of Lothian Road Church, Edinburgh (now Filmhouse) and who had been the moderator of the United Free Church in 1919.

A Watson's Boy

Under my grandfather's auspices I finished my schooling at George Watson's College, Edinburgh. It was a traditional classical education, with rather more attention paid to the trees than to the wood. Indeed, there was one Greek play where we had to learn 300 words which only occurred there and nowhere else in the whole of Greek literature! I don't say that I was educated at Watson's, in the proper sense of the term, for not a lot was *drawn out* from me – but while I don't think I learned much, I was certainly brilliantly taught by a most efficient set of teachers. I recall with particular pleasure George Gray for Greek, Ikey Penman for Latin, Jimmy McEwan and Teddy Albert for English. A great deal of folklore was invented about other teachers such as Unky Shaw, Pa Lennie, Nick Collie and Eva Park, and extra-mural literary composition often took the form of extravagant and scurrilous verse and prose in class magazines about these key figures in our lives. Rugby was not compulsory, but figured highly in the schoolboys' set of values, and oh, my thrill at being chosen to play for the First XV! Singing in the choir, treading the boards with the dramatic club, speaking at the literary society, marching on parade with the OTC – all made for busy and happy days.

Relationships were firmly established within your class, within your year and with the other years above and below. These relationships remained intact as time went by. A big boy who was a 'great man' when you were a wee boy remained a great man even if in later life he did not become more than a bus driver; conversely, a boy who was a wee boy when you yourself had become a great man at school remained a wee boy even after he had entered the cabinet.

During World War II we shared the building of what was then our single-sex school with the girls of George Square. *'Oh brave new world, that had such creatures in it!'* Apartheid was rigorously enforced during school hours, but nevertheless here was yet another afternoon activity to add to the list. But in the evenings, there was just one activity – homework. It took more or less all evening, every evening, and it was just accepted as being the natural order of things. There was of course no television, and although my grandfather had a wireless set, it was only once a year that it was switched on, for the King's Christmas Day broadcast to the Empire. Wartime holidays were spent working at forestry or farming camps, and we also usually had a fortnight at Newtonmore, where it was said that there was a professor on every tee and a minister in every bunker. Grandfather himself was a redoubtable golfer, playing every Monday morning at Bruntsfield till he was ninety-one. He was also a strict sabbatarian. On Sundays we did not sing, and we did not whistle. It was taboo to play games, and homework was unthinkable; many subterfuges were therefore required to find the time and place to complete what would otherwise have been unfinished tasks. But Grandfather was a wonderful man, and a great force for good.

The war rumbled on. We accepted that when we reached the age of eighteen we would join the forces and would do so without reservations. Patriotism had been instilled into us from earliest days. No one was worried about war aims, and no one was troubled with conscientious objections. Food was strictly rationed, but I don't remember ever feeling hungry. There was little variety in what we ate, however, and I do remember that at home for pudding we once had three plums each for forty days running. 'Teenagers' had not yet been invented. If they had been, I would have been a hopeless teenager, for I saw nothing to rebel against. It never occurred to me not to conform to the accepted patterns of behaviour, and I left school fully satisfied that Watson's College was an essential part of the civilized world.

A St Andrews student

My two elder brothers went off to the war, but only one came back. Alastair, four years my senior, was killed in Italy while serving with the 5th Mahratta Light Infantry. He had done an Arts degree at St Andrews University before he joined up, and had so impressed me with what a special place St Andrews was that I had to go there myself. So I proudly wore the scarlet gown for four years, starting with classics and, after a three-year interruption on war service, finishing with English and Philosophy.

The classics professors were noted for their peculiar marking systems. Professor Henry, who presided over Latin, or Humanity, as it was properly called, had only two marks, P and F. Professor Rose had a subtler system for his Greek students. His highest mark, which nobody was ever known to have attained, was S, which stood for *satis*, satisfactory. Next to that came VS, *vix satis*, scarcely satisfactory, and somebody once scored a VS+. When the professor returned the first proses we had written for him, he accompanied his NS marks, *non satis*, with the observation: 'Greek prose should flow elegantly and smoothly. Yours flowed with the easy grace of Tiger tanks lumbering through barbed wire with one caterpillar off.' And irony was never far away either from Professor Nisbet, who commanded the OTC. After inspecting the first parade he drily remarked, 'The turn-out, gentlemen, was execrable, but well up to the usual standard.'

The charm of St Andrews in these days was its small size and intimate atmosphere. The men students tended to come from Fife, Angus and Perthshire, and the women students from Surrey. But wherever we came from, firm friendships were quickly set up, and have lasted a lifetime. This, I think, was the best thing about St Andrews. Then came the dawning of a sense of reverence and of irreverence. You felt brushed by the sweep of history, and stood in awe at the vast store of life and learning around you, but at the same time you couldn't help noticing a vast comic potential in much of what went on. Irreverence, of course, was at the heart of student songs, shows and magazines, and there was a lot of it going about. I made friends early on with Alastair Reid, a fellow son of the manse, who had a gentle and whimsical nature, and an already mature sense of reverence and irreverence. After graduating we lost touch, but fifteen years later he phoned me out of the blue. 'Where are you, Alastair?' I asked, 'and what are you doing?' 'I live on Majorca,' he replied, 'and I write poetry.' This made me feel very humble and very square, because I realized I was a lawyer and lived in Edinburgh.

Alastair Reid went on to receive international acclaim as a poet. He came up to St Andrews as a muscular Christian but when he came back after his war service he had become a muscular aesthete, and may be the only poet who in his time had a trial at full back for the Scottish rugby team. I was sad to find he had lost faith, but at the same time secretly admired his adventurous spirit in being able to change his sense of direction.

St Andrews has many traditional rituals in which we all happily took part – the Bejant Skite, Raisin Monday, the walk to the end of the pier after chapel and the Kate Kennedy procession. This latter is a marvellous annual affair, in which are represented all the famous people connected with the University and the town through the centuries – kings, queens, churchmen, scholars, golfers. At the stroke of two the great doors of St Salvator's Chapel swing open and, bearing his cross, St Andrew himself leads out the ghostly procession in a slow and dignified parade round the town. It is all in honour of the lady Katherine Kennedy, niece of the Bishop who was one of the founders of the University in 1412. Kate was believed to have been good and kind to the poor students of her day, and, if nothing else, is celebrated as an enduring symbol of the springtime of life. She travels in a carriage at the end of the procession with her uncle, and in my time she was played by the bejant (first-year male student) judged to be the best-looking by the senior students in the Kate Kennedy Club – after inspecting the entire first year men one by one! The costumes worn by the 100-odd students who take part in the procession have always been magnificent, and those who have their own real beards are readily distinguished from those wearing false ones. I played the part of the St Andrews poet R.F. Murray one year and the next year the part of Pope Benedict XIII, who granted the bull to authorize the foundation of the University, and whose private name, Pedro da Luna, always made me think of a South American band leader. Kate's retinue includes her jester and her bard, who has to write a celebratory poem. One year the bard portrayed Kate as the encompasser of all student life, the poem including the lines *'All that you saw and all you did not see, I am them all, I am Kate Kennedy'*. All you did not see – and there was a lot I personally did not see. I did not see that my attitudes and prejudices were unchanging. I did not have a sufficiently rigorous mind to follow out philosophical, theological or political arguments wherever they led, perhaps because I feared their conclusions would be uncomfortable. I did not become 'one of the boys', although I longed to be one.

All that you saw – well, Kate has seen a lot of changes, even since my time. Gowns are seldom seen, but although we were not required to wear our scarlet undergraduate gowns, everyone in fact did so, and did so all the time – as well as being decorative they were functional, keeping out the North Sea haar. Nowadays, it seems as if getting to the pub is the big thing in student life, but it was not so in 1943, when there was no pub culture. For one thing, we couldn't afford it, and for another, there were endless coffee shops in which to play at a sort of café society. The idea of living in a flat had not yet arrived. Personally I would not have wanted to do so, and would have considered it a dreadful waste of time to have to go out shopping for foodstuffs and cook my own meals. If you did not live in a residence you lived in a 'bunk' and were looked after by a 'bunkwife', local words for what were known elsewhere as 'digs' and 'landladies'.

St Andrews used to be known as the singing University, and I would be seriously downcast to think that students can no longer be found at a 'Gaudie', the St Andrews word for a singsong, derived from the timeless and universal student song 'Gaudeamus igitur iuvenes dum sumus' (Let us rejoice, therefore, while we are young). It could indeed be a very joyful life, and it never occurred to us that it would ever come to an end. I rejoiced particularly in the lectures of the two marvellous English teachers I had, Professor Blyth Webster and Richard Logan. They each reminded me of a line in *Beowulf* where the poet refers to Beowulf making a speech, but put it this way: '*Then Beowulf opened his treasure chest of words and drew forth the following ...*' Well, Blyth and Logan drew forth endless jewels from their treasure chests of words, and made us look on English literature as itself a very special treasure chest. But whatever subjects we studied, St Andrews drew forth from us what we had not realized was there, and to that extent we were, literally, educated.

A temporary gentleman

At the end of my first year at St Andrews I was eighteen, so it was time to join up. I was posted to the Scots Guards at Caterham, and joined twenty other youngsters sitting apprehensively in a Nissen hut. Morale was low enough on our first day, but plunged to rock-bottom at the entrance of the sergeant-major. 'Right,' he said (all speeches in the army begin with the word 'Right'), 'My name's McLeary. I'm the sergeant-major. The men say I'm a bastard, and by God, they're right.' That was all; exit sergeant-major. It was pure theatre and had the desired effect: his audience collapsed.

We were not allowed out of barracks for three months. It took that amount of time to lick us into some sort of shape where we might pass for guardsmen in the eyes of the world outside. It involved countless hours of square-bashing, endless shining of brass and boots, and cross-country runs of gruelling length. Flying bombs sailed over the parade ground, but woe betide the guardsman who moved a muscle. We learned how to use rifles, bayonets, bren guns, grenades and mortars, and after six months we were licensed to kill. It had been a tremendously tough training, and I am very glad that I had it, but I was even more glad when it came to an end. Shortly afterwards the war in Europe also came to an end, and I was sent to the Officers Training School in Bangalore, the war in the Far East ending as we sailed down the Red Sea.

Arrival in Bombay meant bananas, which we hadn't seen for five years! After several bunches each, we travelled south to Madras, then west to Bangalore, where we were to be turned into officers and gentlemen. Certainly the living conditions were extremely comfortable there. Indian food was a revelation, and bearers waited on us hand and foot. The whole pace of life became relaxed. We had to learn Urdu, and were happy to find it to be a very user-friendly language. After six months of leisurely training we were due to be commissioned, and had to choose a regiment. Since my brother Alastair and three cousins had all been in the Mahrattas I felt I ought to follow suit. But they were a light infantry regiment, and I had been in the Guards! Eventually I opted for what sounded like the nearest thing to the Guards, the Indian Grenadiers.

It was a good life in the Grinders, as the Indian Grenadiers were affectionately known. We saw a lot of the land – desert, jungle, mountains. We saw ancient temples, travelled on ancient railways, and passed through villages where life had seen little change over 3000 years. We had the extraordinary experience of Indian cinema, which seemed to show just two types of film – 'socials' and 'mammoth mythological masterpieces'. Each art form provided an unceasing background of sitar-accompanied song, which to my uncomprehending western ear always seemed to consist of a range of only four or five notes loosely related to a sort of stretched but slackly strung guitar. India certainly cast a spell. I enjoyed it all – both the sahibs' India and the natives' India – and am only sorry that I was too young to appreciate it properly. Serving in the Indian army seemed to me to be preferable to serving in the British army because of the essentially friendly relations between the officers and men. You could indeed have conversations with Indian soldiers which would have been quite unthinkable with British soldiers. The Indians could speak from the heart, and often enough seemed to talk in poetic language, while their British opposite numbers could find it difficult even to stumble into prose. The newspapers told us about Hindu–Muslim strife but this was something we did not experience in our army life. There were two companies of Hindus and two companies of Muslims in the battalion I was in, but, being united by their common loyalty to the regiment, they all got on perfectly well together.

We were sent to Iraq in August 1946, with a view to forestalling an anticipated Russian invasion of Iran. It was so hot that work started at 5am and finished at 8am. We then retired to sweat it out till the cool of the evening. The Russians then changed their plans, and we returned to India in 1947 to find that the independence movement was well under way. My generation had of course been brought up to regard India as the finest jewel in the crown of the British Empire, but we began vaguely to realize that what we had been taught was the Indian Mutiny of 1857 might in fact turn out to have been the first Indian war of independence. In the towns we became aware of anti-British feeling, but so strong had been our conditioning as schoolboys about the peculiar virtue of all things British that we could not take it seriously. But the movement gathered great pace and eventually it was the battalion of the Grenadiers with which I had served that hauled up the Indian flag over the residency at Lucknow when the Union Jack was lowered for the first time since 1857.

My time in the army came to an end in December 1947. I must say that I had enjoyed the army as an institution. I liked giving orders and I liked having orders given to me. It was a secure system – you knew your place. Provided you didn't have to do any fighting or killing it was a very good life. It had been the equivalent of what would nowadays be called 'a year out' between school and University, except that it had been three and a half years out following my first year at University. So after saying a farewell to arms I returned to St Andrews, and started upon Anglo-Saxon grammar, logic and metaphysics. All too soon graduation day arrived, and I finally had to decide what was to follow.

An uncertain call

With all the exposure to the church which I had had, it was going to be difficult to avoid becoming a minister myself. When I started University life it was certainly my intention to become a minister, and when I finished my arts degree in June 1950 my plan still was to enter New College, Edinburgh as a divinity student that October. But during these three summer months I found myself forced to change my mind. I realized that what I had thought was a call to the ministry was really a sentimental attachment to the church as an institution. I did not have – and never have had – any difficulty in accepting the Christian scheme of things, both its metaphysics and its ethics, on an intellectual level. But I did not have an appropriate level of emotional commitment. If a minister is in some sense a salesman, he is not going to be an effective salesman unless he really believes in the value of what he is selling, and by 'really' I mean heart and soul as well as in the intellect. I later found a useful analogy in the different standards of legal proof as between civil and criminal cases. I have always been able easily to say 'I believe in God ' – *on a balance of probabilities* (the civil standard of proof), but I think that to be a minister one must be able to go further and say 'I believe in God' – *beyond reasonable doubt* (the criminal standard of proof). (Saints and mystics, of course, can go further still, and say 'I know'.)

It was not easy telling my grandfather about my proposed change of direction. But he was always a great support to anyone in time of trouble, and after I had told him that I felt I should study the laws of man instead of the laws of God, he at once arranged for me to see Sir Randall Philip QC, the Procurator of the Church of Scotland, to talk with him about what 'the law' meant, for there had never been any lawyers in the family and we knew nothing about it. What emerged from our conversation was that I should go to the Bar and in the first instance seek an apprenticeship in a firm of solicitors.

2

Parliament House

Learning to be a lawyer

I was called to the Bar in 1953. At that time the standard preparation for life as an advocate consisted of taking a three-year law degree – either an LLB, if a first degree had been taken in another discipline, or a BL if it had not – together with two years' work as an apprentice in a solicitor's office and one year 'devilling' to a senior-junior advocate. The academic and the practical work went on together, so that after an early morning class at the University you went down to the office or to the Advocates' Library to work there until it was time for the late afternoon class at the University.

That was all. Neither aspect was particularly satisfactory. University teaching consisted wholly of lectures, and that at a time when the lecturers themselves had received no training in lecturing. Indeed, one professor was sometimes referred to as the 'reader' in his subject because effectively all he did was to read from the standard textbook. And the nearest thing to a visual aid in the whole of legal education was on a page in the mercantile law textbook, which illustrated various ways in which to cross a cheque. There was a course in the law of evidence and procedure, but nothing at all about advocacy – a subject eminently suitable for application of the army training maxim 'Demonstrate in detail, with squad imitating'. No demonstrations were given, detailed or otherwise, and thus the squad had nothing to imitate. There were no moots or mock trials, there were no tutorials and there was no systematic study of case-law.

The theory was that your practical skills were acquired from your apprenticeship and devilling. Whether this worked in practice largely depended on how actively, if at all, your masters were prepared to train you. I was apprenticed to one of the old-established firms of Writers to the Signet, Tods, Murray & Jamieson, but it did little court work except high-society divorces. It seldom did any High Court criminal work, and Sheriff Court work, criminal or civil, was regarded as an inconvenient embarrassment. It was simply farmed out to lesser firms. Apprentices in these days were often regarded as a convenient form of unskilled labour, and a cost-effective form of labour at that, since the emoluments did not amount to more than £50 per year. The apprentice was used largely as a message boy, sent on errands to Register House and Parliament House. The trouble was that while the apprentice was bound in formal written terms to serve his masters faithfully and diligently, and to abstain 'from bad company and vicious practices' and his masters were bound to teach the apprentice in their profession as solicitors, the masters were only bound to do so 'so far as they know themselves and so far as their apprentice shall be capable to learn'. As a result, the apprentice all too often sank or swam according to his own inner resources. Devilling to an advocate also could be a hit-or-miss process. I devilled to Ian Robertson, later Lord Robertson. He was compact, laid-back, encouraging and reassuring, and I regretted not having asked him to tell me more about the minutiae of advocacy than I did.

Calling day

The actual process of being called to the Bar was picturesque. You were required to write a thesis in Latin on a text from Roman law. If the 'examinators' found it to be of an acceptable standard, they would write on it the word '*Impugnetur*' (Let it be assailed). You were then publicly and orally examined on it, being questioned in Latin, and having to answer in Latin. This sounds a formidable undertaking, but in fact it was an agreeable charade. Yes, you did write a thesis in Latin, but you simply copied out one which had been written 200 years previously, when intrants were indeed required to compose their own. Yes, you were questioned in Latin, on three propositions relating to the thesis, but you had chosen the propositions yourself, and you yourself had also composed the three questions and the answers to them. You wrote your questions on slips of paper and gave them to three advocates who had agreed to attend the 'examination'. It used to make me think of the afternoon of Christmas Day in ancient Rome, with Christmas cracker jokes being read out one after the other. But on the other hand it was a very impressive ceremony – what could be more pure or precious than the sight of young men in white ties and tails engaging in Latin debate at eleven o'clock in the morning?

I remember an occasion when one of the three questioners did not turn up. The intrant stated the first of his propositions and waited expectantly for the appropriate question, but silence ensued. Silence continued to ensue. What was the Dean of the Faculty of Advocates, Sir John Cameron, who was presiding at the examination, to do? Fortunately for him, the Professor of Roman Law, Matthew Fisher QC, happened to be attending this examination; and obviously, if anyone could extemporize an appropriate question in Latin, he would be the very man. So the Dean turned to the Professor and invited him to question the intrant. Silence, however, continued to ensue. When it had almost become unbearable, the Professor at last gasped a one-word question '*Cur?*' (Why?). I would like to think that the intrant replied with an equally brilliant answer '*Quia!*' (Because!), but whatever he did say was lost in the roars of applause which greeted the Professor's gallant question.

Thereafter the ballot box was produced. All the members of the Faculty of Advocates who were present had to insert an unseen hand and drop a ball into it. Since there were no black balls it could be thought that this too was a charade, but there were in fact two drawers marked 'Yes' and 'No' into which the balls might be dropped, if you knew of their existence. Once you did know of their existence you knew to twist your hand to the top of the open 'Yes' drawer; but first-timers at this ballot box, not knowing that they would be blackballing an intrant by dropping a white ball into the wrong drawer, could easily do so by mistake. When this happened, the Dean would solemnly announce that the intrant had been elected 'by a large majority'. The intrant was then taken in procession before one of the judges in the Outer House of the Court of Session. The court would be adjourned and the Dean would present the intrant and invite the judge to administer the loyal oath and the oath *de fideli administratione* (concerning the faithful carrying out of the office of advocate) to him. That done and, a word of welcome and encouragement having been administered by the judge if he so wished, the intrant had 'passed advocate' and was entitled to appear before all the courts of the land.

It is now quite different. Law students are required to be full-time students, not part-time students and part-time apprentices. Having completed their three-year academic degree, those who are intending to practise as solicitors spend another year at the University taking their practical diploma. But then comes the rub – obtaining a 'traineeship' in a solicitor's firm is not easy. There are far more people seeking traineeships than there are places for them, if only because the apprentice's nominal pittance has been replaced by the trainee's real remuneration, modest enough, but a not inconsiderable added burden to be borne by those solicitors' firms which can afford it. Yet the fact that firms now have to pay their trainees properly means that their trainees are usually properly trained, and the firms may get value for the money they have to pay them.

Things are much improved too for the aspiring advocate. Devilling continues as before, but the Faculty of Advocates now provides its own training courses as well. It has also introduced refresher courses for those in practice. In-service training is in fact a growth industry. Primarily aimed at the solicitor side of the profession, endless courses, conferences, seminars and workshops take place on all manner of topics. Further, there are now several textbooks on advocacy, none of which was available in 1953.

I would accordingly like to think that if I had had the training available today I would not have been the ridiculously unprepared advocate I was when I started. Indeed, I well remember the embarrassment of my first appearance in a criminal case in the High Court. I knew that you were expected to open the proceedings by standing up and saying that you appeared for the accused, so I did so, and then sat down. I was then aware of the clerk of court looking pointedly at me and whispering what sounded like 'Here to your plea'. I assumed that he meant me to say this, so I stood up again and said, 'I'm here to my plea.' This met with amazed looks from clerk and judge, and it was only later that the clerk explained that what I should have said was that my client 'adheres to his plea'. This sort of thing would not have happened if today's wide-ranging training had then been available, or if High Court trials had taken place then with even one-quarter of the frequency they do now.

The bread-and-butter of divorce

Before criminal cases became so widespread it was divorce which was the provider of bread-and-butter for the young advocate setting out on his career. Until 1988 all divorce cases involved a hearing in court, and the Court of Session was the only court. The rules of evidence were strictly observed, some judges being even more strict than others, so much so that instead of the standard four-guinea fee for conducting a divorce proof, it was felt that a proof before Lord Wheatley should rate a fee of five guineas as danger money and before Lord Guthrie one of six guineas. On the other hand, before Lord Migdale it sometimes seemed that it was only necessary to say 'My Lord, may I introduce my client Mrs So-and-so?' and then sit down, so keen was he to question the witnesses himself.

But Lord Guthrie could unbend. By way of a party-piece at a legal dinner where he was the guest of honour I gave a short musical talk on the undefended divorce for desertion. In such a case two things had to be established. Firstly, that the pursuer's wife had indeed left him. This was well illustrated by one of the songs from the mid-1930s hit parade 'Dinner for one, please, James'. 'Close madam's room, we've parted' went the lyric, and it was clear that there was to be no return. Secondly, it was necessary to establish that if the defender had returned, the pursuer would have been *willing to adhere* – i.e. willing to take her back again. This element in a divorce proof often involved the finest stretching of the truth, but no such difficulty was suggested by the song 'I wonder what's become of Sally?', finishing as it did with the gloriously reassuring lines: 'Wherever she has gone, wherever she may be, if no one wants her now, please send her back to me. I'll always welcome back my Sally, that old gal of mine.' Having sung these two songs, I was amazed, but delighted, to hear Lord Guthrie say in a loud whisper, 'Decree!'

Desertion for a period of three years was one of the principal grounds for divorce, the other two most commonly founded on being adultery and cruelty. All three grounds were based on the concept of the 'matrimonial offence', where one party was said to be the guilty party and the other the innocent. This concept was abandoned by the Divorce (Scotland) Act 1976, and there is now only one ground for divorce – irretrievable breakdown of the marriage, not necessarily implying fault on either side (although, of course, the breakdown may in fact have been brought about by desertion, adultery or cruelty). Proof of adultery had to be beyond reasonable doubt, and it was always a comfort to be able to produce a birth certificate to show that a child had been born of an adulterous liaison; this was commonly referred to as 'a nice, clean adultery'. It was also a comfort to be able to found on the presumption of adultery if the defender and paramour had been discovered *solus cum sola in loco suspecto* (a man alone with a woman in a suspicious setting): this presumption was even stronger if they were found to be *nudus cum nuda in loco suspecto* (the same, with no clothes on).

In divorce on the grounds of cruelty it was necessary to prove that the pursuer's health had suffered as a result of the defender's behaviour towards her. In a case I had where a school teacher had married a farmer there was no doubt that the pursuer's health had suffered grievously. Her doctor said that three months after the marriage she had changed in appearance from a happy confident girl to one whom he at first thought was in an advanced stage of a wasting disease. What had brought this about? One of her minor complaints was that her husband was extraordinarily mean, and it appeared that he had used the freewill offering envelopes he had been given at their church as pay packets for his farmworkers. But her major complaint was of excessive sexual demands, and her husband was asked in cross-examination by my senior, Robert Taylor QC, 'Despite the fact that you must have seen how your wife's health had deteriorated, did you nevertheless continue to have sexual relations with her right up till the time she left?' His reply began, unexpectedly, 'Well now, I think she left about five o'clock ...'

Despite a valiant rearguard action by the Faculty of Advocates to have divorce kept in the Court of Session, it was eventually made available in the Sheriff Court, and soon became almost entirely a Sheriff Court process. The most obvious advantage was in cost. Previously, if a pursuer lived outside Edinburgh, he would have to employ three lawyers – his local solicitor, an Edinburgh solicitor and an advocate. Further, he would have to travel to Edinburgh for the Saturday morning hearing. Now, in almost all cases, a divorce is simply done on paper without a court appearance, requiring only one solicitor – apart, that is, from cases involving no children and no dispute about money, where divorce is commonly done on a 'Do-it-yourself' form-filling basis.

A planning inquiry

My first civil case, however, was not a court case at all. I was instructed by Edinburgh Corporation to appear for them at a planning enquiry into their proposal to build houses on the lower slopes of Arthur's Seat beside Dunsappie Loch. Such enquiries were a fruitful source of income to the Bar, as senior counsel were often appointed to conduct them as well as being briefed to appear at them. This enquiry was conducted by Mr James Walker QC, then Vice-Dean of Faculty and who later became Lord Walker, a most genial and learned judge. Mr C.W.G. Guest QC, later Dean of Faculty and thereafter Lord Guest, a judge in the House of Lords, was my senior. Opposing us were Mr R.A. Bennett, Advocate, my future wife's brother-in-law, and Mr John G. Gray, a most energetic solicitor; they represented the 'Dunsappie Committee', one of the many *ad hoc* amenity groups for which Edinburgh became famous – through opposing any development proposals which the Corporation might make. As Mr Guest and I had been instructed by the Corporation we were entertained to lunch in the City Chambers, and there I first heard the euphemism 'refreshment'. Asked by a city officer if I would like a refreshment, I replied in my innocence that I was not tired and did not require to be refreshed. It was only after a number of puzzled looks from the officer that I realized that he was offering me a drink. Refreshed or not, however, our case did not succeed, and Arthur's Seat escaped the hands of a developer.

Nobody starved at the Scottish Bar

It used to be said that nobody starved at the Scottish Bar. This was true, and there was indeed a lot of money for old rope going about in the 1950s. There was much formal procedure which required the drafting or signature by counsel of various short documents at three or four guineas a time. Further, the two-counsel rule was rigorously applied. If a client wished to have senior counsel representing him, or had senior counsel wished upon him by his solicitor, junior counsel had to be instructed also – to try to ensure that the senior did not overlook anything at consultation or in examining witnesses in court. Juniors were also expected to prepare their cases fully as a back-up in case their seniors fell by the wayside. This only happened once in my experience, when on opening our case in the appeal court my senior announced – to my alarm – that as he had lost his voice to such an extent that it would be an impertinence for him to continue, his junior would now address their Lordships!

And if, in the short term, life at the Bar seemed to be getting nowhere, there was comfort in the knowledge that in the long term almost everyone could expect to 'get a job' by the age of fifty – as judge, sheriff or chairman of a tribunal. For there were about eighty such jobs all told, and about eighty practising advocates. What the prospects are nowadays I do not like to think, because the number of practising advocates has grown fourfold, while the number of jobs has not.

With such a small number in practice in the 1950s, the Bar was a very intimate body. Whether or not we were learned, we were certainly friends. The coffee room was a daily reminder of this. There shop was happily talked, horror stories of judges at their most overbearing were exchanged, advice was sought and readily given on tricky points of law and practice, 'interesting information', a euphemism for gossip, was passed round and, occasionally, candidatures for parliamentary seats were traded. The Bar has always been a stepping-stone towards Parliament, but it was not just the purely politically minded who sought candidatures – for service to the party (usually the Tory party) had always been a stepping stone to advancement in government service, as crown counsel, sheriff or judge. But for those with such personal rather than political ambitions, the concept of a 'safe seat' took on an entirely different meaning from the usual one, and was one where there was no possibility of being elected! For election would have interfered immeasurably with professional practice and social life in Edinburgh; but the fact that the advocate had nobly shown an unpopular party's flag in an unwinnable seat would not be forgotten when that party eventually came to power. So the theory ran, and certainly there were a number of unlikely candidates standing for unlikely seats.

The working life of the Bar was held together by the four advocates' clerks, Jack Scotland, Johnny Speirs, Murray Scobie and Gilbert McWhannel. All newly qualified advocates became a member of one or other of their 'stables', usually joining the one to which their devil-master belonged. Solicitors normally gave work to their favourite advocates, but where first-choices were not available, solicitors relied on the clerks for obtaining the services of an appropriate advocate – the clerks knew who were the horses for the courses. It was also the clerks' duty to promote the interests of beginners, and at the other extreme, where fashionable seniors could expect fees in excess of the norm, to negotiate such fees. The clerks were a great clearing-house for the Faculty, their ears were close to the ground, they knew what was happening and they helped to make it happen. It was of course very necessary to maintain a good relationship with one's clerk; and the relationship was normally an intimate one, if only because every time a solicitor paid an advocate a fee for a piece of work he had to pay that advocate's clerk a fee of one-twentieth of the advocate's fee, whether or not the clerk had actually done anything.

Civil work

The work was very largely civil, not criminal. Junior counsel had to attend to all the written pleadings, which were both the glory and the shame of the Scottish system of civil procedure. Each party's case had to be written out in meticulous detail. Averments had to be made of facts which it was intended to prove, and propositions in law set down which these facts were expected to support. The glory lay in the comprehensive coverage of the whole case, the logical progression of thought and the elegance of its expression. The shame lay in the emphasis placed on the written pleadings, and the fine-combing to which they were subject – this with a view to finding something not quite right about them so as to ground a plea to their relevancy.

'Relevancy' was indeed a concept which dominated the system. Pleadings were irrelevant if, assuming that all the facts averred were proved, a good case in law was not made out. Pleadings were also irrelevant if there was insufficient specification of the facts averred. Nit-picking debates on relevancy were a feature of everyday practice, and some practitioners were past-masters at thinking up absurd but just plausible points to demonstrate that their opponent's case was irrelevant. If a relevancy plea was successful, the case was dismissed there and then without any evidence having to be led. Often enough one felt that the court was not deciding the actual case between the parties, but the apparent case between the parties on their pleadings, which was not necessarily the same thing. Perfectly good cases could fail because of technical deficiencies in the pleadings: justice could thereby founder in the mechanics of the law.

Some defenders' counsel took pleas to the relevancy as a matter of course, without bothering too much as to whether or not they were justified. If nothing else, they served as a delaying device, because the case could not proceed to proof (the hearing of evidence) until the question of relevancy had been disposed of. They could also cause much anxiety to the pursuer's counsel, who had to anticipate what esoteric point his adversary would seek to make at the debate about what seemed to him to be his perfectly sound pleadings. Over the years, however, the courts put less and less stress on the necessity of perfect pleadings, which was all to the good, and eventually, in 1992, a major change to the system was made – for it was provided that notice had to be given in advance of the basis on which a plea to the relevancy had been taken. No longer did an advocate have to go into court for a debate without knowing what points would be taken against him! Further, a debate would only be allowed if the judge decided that a *prima facie* arguable case on the relevancy had been put forward. This was a great step forward. The immense amount of time and expense wasted in hopeless debates on hopeless points was avoided, and so too was the needless worry on the part of advocates whose cases would otherwise have been under unknown forms of attack.

Much time also used to be consumed in argument as to whether the inquiry into the facts was to be before a jury or a judge. This question usually arose in reparation cases where pursuers had suffered personal injuries. Pursuers hoped to have a jury, defenders hoped to have a judge, as it was believed that a jury would not concern itself overmuch with the law or the evidence.

The theory, at its crudest, was that all a pursuer had to do in a case where he had lost his hands in an accident at work and was suing his employers for damages, was to go into the witness-box, say to the jury 'Look, no hands' and the jury would say 'give him the money'; and as part of the application of this theory, objection was often taken by a pursuer's counsel to teachers or other professional persons being on the jury, since it was feared that they might be intelligent enough actually to listen to the evidence and to apply the law in which the judge instructed them, namely, that damages could only be awarded if the jury was satisfied on the evidence that negligence on the part of the employers had been proved. The theory also provided, of course, that judges *would* listen to the evidence and apply the law; but, other things being equal, some judges were thought in general to favour pursuers, and some to favour defenders. It was not unknown for a case to have been set down before one judge thought likely to be unfavourable, and a motion then to be made for an adjournment in the hope of obtaining another of a different disposition. If this might be described as a form of gamesmanship, it would only be because the contesting of a case in court could be, and often was, described as a game. I never liked this idea. It might be thought of as a game by the lawyers concerned, but for the litigants it could be a deadly serious business.

In your first year or two as an advocate you spent much time going from court to court, watching how various judges behaved and how certain advocates performed. It was always a great experience to hear one of the leading seniors going hammer and tongs at a witness or, for that matter, at a judge. You marvelled at their style, their self-confidence, their aggression, and wondered if you could ever achieve such poise yourself. They seemed to know it all, and if they did not, they were remarkably good at giving the impression that they did. They appeared to belong to another world entirely, one where they could treat judges as their equals, sometimes as their intimates and sometimes as rather backward children who required allowances to be made for them.

The good and the great

The two giants of the Bar in 1953 were R.P. Morrison and Jock Cameron. Both were extremely quick workers – they had to be, such was the volume of work which came their way – and both were immediate commanders of close attention from all whom they addressed. Although both were approachable, it was by no means easy for a beginner to speak to the great men, because the convention was that you addressed all your brethren by name, never prefixed by 'Mister', and preferably by their first names. I certainly could not bring myself to call Morrison 'R.P.' if I had occasion to speak to him, nor could I possibly have called the great Jock 'Cameron'.

Jock Cameron, of course, became a quite outstanding Dean of Faculty. In the army I had found that some commanding officers were technically efficient and others sought to be regarded as 'one of the boys'. It was very difficult to be both. But as the Faculty's commanding officer Jock *was* both, and was extremely good at being both. You knew when he was on parade and you knew when he was off parade. Magnificent when on parade in court or in Faculty meetings, he was a marvellous companion off parade. He was involved in many aspects of national life outside the law courts and was an active promoter of the arts. When with him you realized that you were privileged to be in the presence of one of the supreme Scotsmen of the twentieth century.

His vice-deans were James Walker, affable, quizzical, avuncular, and T.P. McDonald, calm, straightforward, homely, and the first of those of my time whom I would describe as having been passed over for no apparent reason for well-deserved promotion to the Bench. Another whom one might have expected to see on the Bench was Hector McKechnie, but perhaps he was too much of a 'character' to have played the part of a 'senator' – as the judges were properly called, being technically senators of the College of Justice (advocates and solicitors were simply members). Randall Philip was another who could well have been made a judge. Small and rotund, he nevertheless had much gravitas about him, yet was kindly withal, being sometimes referred to as 'the amiable armadillo' or simply as 'the Puffin'. Among others who in my opinion should have been made judges but were not were Stanley Gimson and Robert Reid, both very clever and witty men, and Ronnie Bennett, who was certainly the quickest worker I ever came across.

Of all those who did grace the Court of Session Bench in my time, my favourite judge was Lord Justice Clerk Thomson, to whom, alas, I can claim no relationship. He was relaxed and humorous, in contrast to his contemporary Lord President Cooper. Both were kindly men, however, and both were great judges. But George Thomson had the gift of being able to write eminently readable judgments, which combined technical language with down-to-earth and almost racy prose. At the other end of the scale in readability was Lord (Sandy) Mackay, the living embodiment of the maxim 'Why use one word where ten will do?'. Lord Patrick I always saw as a grave Roman senator, unworldly and wholly reliable; and I saw Lord Sorn as Sir Malcolm Sargent – a debonair conductor with a twinkle in his eye. I used to while away dull moments by trying to see the Court of Session judges as orchestral players, deciding which instruments it would be appropriate for each to play. For instance, I could see Lord Clyde with a piccolo, Lord Wheatley with a trombone, Lord Blades with a bassoon, Lord Avonside with an oboe, Lord Kissen winding up a horn, Lord (Douglas) Johnston plucking a violin, Lord Strachan playing a cello and Lord Grant sawing a double bass.

Lord President Clyde was the quintessential quick Greek, restlessly darting from one point to another and not easy to please. His successor was the solidly Roman Lord Emslie, a president of military bearing and efficiency. I enjoyed Lord Stott's abilities and idiosyncrasies so much that when once asked if I had any ambitions, I replied, 'Yes, to write a civil judgment which would be overturned by the First Division, Lord Stott dissenting – and then unanimously restored by the House of Lords!'

Chris Guest succeeded Jock Cameron as Dean of Faculty. He was a rather austere-looking man, but carried great authority in his presence; you felt he could only have been a lawyer, and as a judge he went on to sit in the House of Lords. He in turn was succeeded both as Dean and in the Lords by Jim Shaw, who, by contrast, you felt could have been many things, not least the musician that he actually was in his spare time. These three – Cameron, Guest, Shaw – had all added to the stature of the office of Dean, and when the next vacancy arose it so happened that there were three candidates, each of whom was also of outstanding stature. They were Harald Leslie, Ian Shearer and Jack Hunter, and they were very different men. Harald Leslie had a gloriously rich Scots voice, and was universally beloved as a good man. It was entirely appropriate that he should have been appointed Lord High Commissioner to the General Assembly of the Church of Scotland. Ian Shearer was Hanoverian in appearance but often seemed to be wearing his wig as if it were the scrum cap of an imposing lock forward. He was as tough as they come, not easy to get close to, but extremely effective in court. Jack Hunter, a handsome man, had a happy smile and a ready laugh. He always made me think of a swashbuckling buccaneer, but he was a master of detail, never happier in court than when dealing with complicated productions: 'Just look at production 56/6(c). How does that compare with production 34/9 and production 41/9(d)?'

Despite their very different personalities, each of them would have been equally impressive as Dean. The Faculty was deeply divided on the matter of whom to choose and the matter was eventually resolved by not choosing any of them but by bringing in and electing an outside compromise candidate, Ian Fraser, who, in his own way, a gently persuasive way, made an excellent Dean. The other great Dean that I should mention was Alec Thomson, also, alas, no relation. He was busy and businesslike, chairing the committee which led to a radical revisal of Scottish criminal procedure, but always radiated good cheer, and was an unpretentious friend to all.

Another much-loved friend to all was the great criminal practitioner of my time, Lionel Daiches QC. He was small in stature but immense in his eloquence and wit, a silver-tongued Demosthenes if ever there was one. He was always dapper in appearance, and I hugely enjoyed the story he told against himself of attending a conference in the deep south of America in his bowler hat, black jacket and striped trousers, handing his hat to a coal-black mammy cloakroom attendant and finding her arm like a great elephant's trunk going round his waist while she said, 'Honeychile, Ah is a-gonna look after you, 'caz Ah can see you is from outta town.'

The Friendly Faculty

Friendliness was a key feature of the family life of the Faculty. Everyone knew everyone, and although there was competition, it was without malice. Bar dinners took place when there were special birthdays to be celebrated, the most famous being that of the centenarian Sheriff George Wilton in 1962. He had become well-known for championing the cause of a Scottish medical missionary, Dr Henry Faulds, whom he recognized as the pioneer promoter of fingerprint identification. At the age of 100 Sheriff Wilton was still perfectly capable of making an appropriate speech and indeed brought the house down by apologising for wearing a grey tweed suit with a black bow tie. 'My dinner jacket wore out when I was ninety-eight,' he said, 'and in all the circumstances I did not think it was worthwhile to buy another.' Mainly, however, Bar dinners took place once or twice a year, the occasion for them being when anyone became engaged to be married. Speeches were of course made by the presiding Dean and by the marriage celebrant, and there would often in addition be speeches on seriously funny legal themes, such as 'The Silver Jubilee of *Donoghue v Stevenson*' or 'Sewers, noxious fumes and nuisances'. Songs were always sung, the three songsters being Cameron Miller, Arthur Duffes and myself. Cameron Miller, of whom more later, became legendary, and fortunately gramophone records were made of his Bar Dinner Songs, preserving them for posterity.

Arthur Duffes was a remarkable character. Of a military presence and ramrod straight, he returned to practise at the Bar at an advanced age after serving as a Sheriff Principal and a National Insurance commissioner. So senior was he that almost every judge was junior to him. He was one of the very last advocates to be entitled to borrow books from the National Library for home reading, having been a member of Faculty before 1924, when the Faculty ceased to be responsible for what became the National Library; what he frequently borrowed, however, were ancient comics for his granddaughters to read! But every inch a courtly Edwardian gentleman, he always sang, in a quavering voice, the same song – 'Ae fond kiss'. Equally senior to Duffes was Lillie. 'Jake' Lillie had a distinctly melancholy air to him, and it was difficult to think of him having ever sung at all, love songs or otherwise, or having ever made a joke.

I sang what I hoped were funny songs at the piano. I could not sing well enough to sing seriously nor play the piano well enough to play seriously, so what I always tried to do was to sing funny songs to my own accompaniment – an art form where you don't require a particularly high standard of either singing or playing, but just hope to get by on the jokes. Schnozzle Durante's 'Lost Chord' was a favourite, and others I particularly enjoyed doing were 'The People's Friend', 'I wanna go back to Morningside', 'The Mexican Hat Dance', 'Skin' and 'The Last Tram'.

When I think of the friendly activities that most advocates became involved in, I think of golf. Golf is a game with which I have had a lifelong love-and-hate affair, and I am more or less convinced that man's inhumanity to man is nothing compared to golf's inhumanity to man. But the Bench and Bar Foursomes at Muirfield were usually very happy affairs. I remember a memorable scene when Lillie and Duffes were on opposing sides. Lillie was about to putt, and Duffes stood at the edge of the green, idly swinging his putter in his hand. Lillie addressed the ball, then removed his club from the ball, straightened up and said, 'I'll thank you, Duffes, not to play the fool while I am putting.' The thought of Duffes playing the fool in any way was so impossible to entertain that all those who heard this rebuke were quite unable to keep straight faces.

Matches took place every year against the Bench and Bar of England and the Bench and Bar of Ireland. I once went with the team to play the Northern Irish at Portrush, having been taken along more to strengthen the singing end of the Scottish team than the golfing end, as our team had been defeated in the after-dinner singing at the previous encounter. Sticking in my memory of the after-dinner proceedings was the competition in which the Irish players engaged to see which of them could say the words 'Around the world in eighty days' in the most powerful Irish brogue. The results were amazing – a series of massive and irresistible assaults on these unfortunate vowels and diphthongs!

On the golf course I had the equally amazing experience of playing with the first Lord Milligan and Stewart Bell in a two-ball fivesome. Now the much-loved Lord Milligan, splendid track athlete though he had been, was not a technically efficient golfer. Indeed, when there was enquiry as to the standard of any particular golfer, the reply was sometimes made, 'He comes somewhere between Jack Nicklaus and Lord Milligan!' But at the same time Lord Milligan was a superb gamesman. One of our opponents had a pronounced waggle. Now the waggle, a familiar preliminary to any shot from tee to green, is designed to reduce tension, the arch-destroyer of golf shots. This Irishman waggled so much that counting the waggles became unavoidable. After about twenty waggles he felt able to hit the shot, and did so with, usually, erratic results. On one occasion, after his side had unexpectedly won a hole and he was about to tee up at the next hole prior to driving, or waggling, off again, Lord Milligan said in a loud whisper, 'Now Stewart, you look well over to the right, and Nigel, you look well over to the left, and with any luck we may see where it goes!' This, of course, did nothing to reduce the Irishman's tension, the twenty waggles became forty, and they lost the hole.

The Harpic Players

What became in effect the Faculty Comic Opera company was the Harpic Players (clean round the bend). The company consisted of advocates and their wives and sweethearts, supplemented by a number of marvellously talented people from outside the Faculty. It performed in large New Town drawing rooms, usually those of Sheriff Principal Robert Taylor QC and Gordon Coutts QC. There was no charge for admission and no collection for charity – we just performed for fun and for the party afterwards, three nights at a time and with hand-picked audiences. We always performed what we liked to think of as musical Shakespeare. The scripts contained a passing resemblance to familiar Shakespearean plots, and *the dramatis personae* occasionally resembled the originals. The general level of the shows can be deduced from the fact that in the Harpic version of *Hamlet* there were no grave-diggers, but there were two gold-diggers, one called Rosie Krantz and the other called Gilda Stern.

The company was formed about 1952 by Cameron Miller, who had been the Sheriff at Fort William and by John Wilson QC, who became one of the Sheriffs at Edinburgh. Early on, Cameron Miller became the sole scriptwriter, and he was partnered as composer by a solicitor friend of the Wilsons, Johnston Moffat. They were a complete Gilbert and Sullivan pair, Cameron with an infinite capacity for writing witty verse, and Johnston turning out an unending flow of graceful or pulsating but always utterly singable melody. Together they put Shakespeare into a completely new light; altogether over the years there were some thirty-seven performances of the dozen different operas, from *King Leer* to *The Compost*, from *King Charles II Part 3* to *Omlet, Prince of Eigg*.

I joined the company in 1955 as rehearsal pianist in succession to Anne Mackenzie Stuart. Her husband Jack, later to become President of the European Court of Justice, was then one of the juvenile leads. He would modestly describe himself as almost tone-deaf, but he gave a convincing Rex Harrison-type rendition of whatever songs he was required to sing. Many other distinguished members of Faculty appeared on stage with the company, including Lord Cowie, Lord Prosser, Sheriff Principal Robert Reid, Sheriff Principal Stanley Gimson, Sheriff Hector Maclean, Lionel Daiches QC and Hugh Campbell QC, as did the wives of Sheriff Morris Rose, Sheriff A.B. Wilkinson and Hugh Campbell. From outside the Faculty came the unforgettable Giles sisters, and also Alison Bent, Astrid Chalmers-Watson, Iain, Fiona and Mairead Maclaren, Lolo Magnusson and Rosemary Walker. Apart from Johnston Moffat, the pianists were Sheriff James Fiddes QC and John Mitchell QC. Lastly, and no one would ever say leastly, mention must be made of the indefatigable stage manager, Sheriff Martin Mitchell.

What fun it all was! There was never enough room to accommodate all who wanted to see the shows, although it was traditional to insult the audience and the audience knew this. The closing chorus usually went along these lines:–

> Yet we hope you've enjoyed your evening And we leave you with a sigh;
> We are always glad to see you, But we really can't think why.
> We are the great Shakespearians, Unblemished and free from vice.
> We charge you no admission, And you're exactly worth the price.

It was also traditional to poke cheerful fun at the Court of Session judges, and to invite them to attend to join in the fun, which they did. Nobody would pretend that the shows were of any particular artistic merit – indeed, the Harpics' motto was 'our best is not too good', but standing out over everything was Cameron Miller's amazing bass voice which could plumb depths otherwise undiscovered by mortal man, and his endless ability to create rhyming couplets, laced with outrageous puns, which brought joy and delight to so many Faculty members and followers over so many years.

My lasting debt to the Harpic Players is that my involvement with them brought me my wife. One year one of the girls had dropped out of the company and a replacement was being sought. Cameron Miller's twelve-year-old daughter told him that her music teacher at Lansdowne House School, Lolo Magnusson, was a good singer, 'but, mind you, she's quite old, probably about twenty-five'. As I happened to be the producer of the Harpic show that year he asked me to audition her. I went to his house at the appointed time and rang the bell. The door was opened by Cameron's daughter. She said to me, and I quote her words *verbatim*: 'My music teacher's here tonight. She's very pretty. Marry her.' Out of the mouths of babes and sucklings! I can safely say that Lolo's singing was the most beautiful sound I had and have ever heard; she passed the audition to such effect that we in time did marry, and have lived happily ever after.

Home and away

I have nothing against criminal legal aid except that it wasn't around when I was around. Indeed, it was only shortly before I was called to the Bar that advocates appearing for the poor in criminal cases (and most accused persons were poor) even received their travelling expenses. My practice often took me out of town, particularly to the Sheriff Court in Dundee and the High Court in Glasgow. I remember to my embarrassment a classic Freudian slip I perpetrated in one of my early High Court cases. After what I had hoped was a powerfully persuasive speech to the jury demonstrating my client's innocence, I concluded by saying, 'And so, ladies and gentlemen, I would invite you with confidence to find my client guilty.' Then I added (is 'lamely' the right word?), 'I'm sorry, I mean not guilty.' Not surprisingly, the jury accepted my first invitation.

I always liked to visit the scene of the crime or the litigation so as to feel more 'at home' with my client's case. I was once briefed to appear for two old ladies who were objectors to an application by the Hibs Supporters Association for a licensed club in Edinburgh's Carlton Terrace. I hoped to paint an alarming picture of the Association's 2000 members, each with his entitled two guests, thus 6000 in all, coming up from Easter Road conjubilant with football song and roaring drunk – and causing havoc in Carlton Terrace's gardens before they had even entered the club at all. In order to experience Hibs supporters at first hand, therefore, I went to watch a match at Easter Road, and visited various nearby pubs afterwards. To my irritation, I found the supporters to be a remarkably orderly and relatively sober body of men! Even so, I am glad to say that the old ladies' cause prevailed, and the club remained at Easter Road.

The General Assembly of the Church of Scotland, I had been told, was the rudest court in the land, with frequent cries of 'Sit down and shut up'. So it was with some trepidation that I addressed the fathers and brethren from the bar of their court on behalf of a Presbytery which did not want a proposed amalgamation of churches to take place. But the members of the Assembly were as well-behaved as the Hibs supporters had been, although it was certainly an odd experience to be liable to be questioned not just by three judges in the civil Appeal Court but by as many as 300 in this ecclesiastical Appeal Court.

I took part in a number of cases for the North of Scotland Hydro-Electric Board, usually inquiries into the siting of overhead lines. Since in law the owner of land owns not only the actual ground on which he stands but all that is below and above it – *a centro usque ad coelum* (a romantic Latin phrase meaning 'from the centre of the earth right up to the very heaven') – the Hydro Board had to get permission from landowners to route their lines over the landowners' ground, and also had to pay them for the right to do so. There was a time in the 1960s when, following a well-publicized case (*Crichel Down*) in which a Government department was held to have ridden roughshod over citizens' private property rights, the Government became so apprehensive of losing further face over this sort of thing that public inquiries were ordered into the most trivial matters. One such inquiry in which I appeared was into the Hydro Board's proposal to route a line over the corner of a farmer's field, which would encroach upon his airspace for about ten yards. The farmer declined to sign the agreement to grant the Board a wayleave through his airspace, for which they were proposing to pay an annual rent of sixpence. Now the farmer had no mains electricity in his farm, and the Board had quoted him a figure of £3000 as the amount he would have to pay them as the cost of installing a supply. Although the two matters were entirely unconnected, he nevertheless felt aggrieved at the disparity between what he was being asked to pay the Board and what the Board was proposing to pay him. So an inquiry was ordered into this proposed sixpenny wayleave. What the outcome was I do not now remember, but the climax of the old farmer's evidence was unforgettable: 'Some of my friends said I'd be daft to sign, and some of my friends said I'd be daft not to sign, and some of my friends said I was just daft onywey!'

I was very impressed with the general efficiency of the Hydro Board, but even Homer nods occasionally, and one Friday night, in a rush to get things finished, they accidentally accepted an offer which they had had no intention of accepting. It was for a Japanese machine for making electricity out of peat: you put peat in at one end, turned the handle, and electricity should have come out of the other. The Board had paid £250,000 for it, but it did not work to their satisfaction, so they decided to sell it. A scrap merchant offered £50, and this was the offer which by mistake was accepted. The Board refused to pay, and the scrap merchant promptly sued them in Inverness Sheriff Court for the apparent breach of contract. After a lengthy proof the Sheriff took the case to *avizandum* – i.e. he went away to think about it before delivering his judgment – and did so for no less than five years, which must be some sort of record. This was not too surprising, as neither side wanted to press the Sheriff to issue a judgment, both sides being likely to emerge badly from it; it was also a difficult case both in fact and in law. What was surprising, however, was that when the Sheriff eventually did issue his judgment he refused to certify the case as having been suitable for the employment of counsel!

Whether home or away, I enjoyed both the academic and the theatrical elements of an advocate's life. Entering the library to begin research on a new case often gave me an almost physical thrill, and it was very satisfying to look up all the possible leads that I could think of which might lead to the answer to the questions put to me in a memorial for my opinion. Often enough the answer could not be a straight yes or no, but had to be clouded with qualifications and provisos. Nevertheless, when I felt assailed by self-doubt I would remind myself that whichever solicitor had asked for the opinion had had sufficient confidence in me to ask me for *my* opinion, and, furthermore, had been prepared to pay for it.

In court, you in effect walked on to the stage of a theatre where a company of actors engaged in a partly scripted partly improvised drama. Examination of your own witnesses was not easy. Although you knew what they were likely to say, you had to be very careful to word your questions so as to bring out the answers you wanted without sounding as if you were 'leading' the witnesses to say what you wanted to hear them say. Cross-examination of the other side's witnesses could be fun, but did not mean that you should examine as if you were cross with them. Best of all was addressing the jury. Styles of advocacy had changed. Oratory directed at the jury had gone out of fashion and had been replaced by one-way conversation, but it was still possible to enliven that conversation with a variety of intonation and gesture, with humour and pathos, and with changing pace and dynamics. It was different, of course, where there was no jury. You could not address a judge as if he were a public meeting. But still there was that sense of theatre, in which he played his part along with the rest of the *dramatis personae*, and it was always very satisfying when you realized that the judge or jury were actually listening to you.

The electricity from peat machine case was my last case at the Bar. I did not apply to become a silk, that is, a senior counsel or Queen's Counsel, for two reasons. I had a perfectly good practice for a junior, but the firms which engaged me did not tend to do the type of work for which senior counsel were then required; and I was aware that I did not possess that aggressive self-confidence which a successful senior should have – the other side's cases often seemed to me to be the more persuasive! So I applied to be appointed a Sheriff, where the essence of the work was considering each side of a case without being predisposed to one side or another.

3

Hamilton Sheriff Court

My colleagues

I was appointed Sheriff in Hamilton and Airdrie in May 1966. In Airdrie I had the great pleasure of having Sheriff Isabel Sinclair as my colleague. As the first ever full-time lady Sheriff she was a delight, both on and off parade. She had been editor of the Women's Page in the *Scottish Daily Express* before she came to the Bar, and not surprisingly had an encyclopedic knowledge of the ways of the world, particularly the Glasgow world in which she had been brought up. She had a lovely sense of humour, and radiated *joie de vivre*: whenever she entered a room, you felt that everyone said to themselves, 'Good, here's Isabel.'

Since lady Sheriffs were a novelty, people were sometimes uncertain of how to address her in court. She enjoyed telling me how she had overheard a mother impatiently 'tutoring' her child who was to be a witness: 'Now Jeannie, just tell yon wumman up there whit ah telt ye tae tell her – ah'm wantin' awa' hame tae get yer dad's tea ready!' Yon wumman scored a notable victory when the celebrated Nicky Fairbairn appeared before her as counsel in one of the first cases she had to hear. He addressed her as 'My Lord'. 'Be so good, Mr Fairbairn,' Isabel said, 'as to address me as "My Lady".' 'No, I'm sorry my Lord,' said Nicky, 'I can't do that, it wouldn't be right.' 'Don't be tiresome, Mr Fairbairn, you should address me as "My Lady".' 'My Lord, that would not be proper, no judge in Scotland has ever been called "My Lady".' 'Mr Fairbairn,' finally said Isabel in exasperation, 'if you're going to persist in this silly behaviour, then, until the end of this case I will address you as "Miss Fairbairn".' I don't know if Nicky ever forgave her for this excellent put-down.

In Hamilton my colleagues were Sheriffs Ian Dickson and Peter Thomson. They were very different people, and did not get on particularly well together, so much so that it was sometimes suggested that I had been sent there to keep the peace between them. But I became fond of both of them, particularly Ian Dickson. He was a man of tremendous energy. He had lost a leg, and I sometimes wondered what on earth he would have been like in terms of volcanic activity if he had had two good legs. Although he loved the Sheriff Court and all its ways and works – indeed it is quite impossible for anyone to think of Hamilton Sheriff Court in the 1960s and 70s without thinking of Ian Dickson as its father-figure – he could be abrupt and imperious in manner. It was said of Sir Winston Churchill that when you first met him you saw all his bad points in your first half-hour with him, and then spent the rest of your life enjoying all his many good ones. So with Ian Dickson. Far too many people, however, only had half an hour with him: I had the privilege of ten years.

Peter Thomson, by contrast, was a large, brooding, easy-going person. He was very pleasant company, but he kept himself very much to himself, and I sometimes felt that I had to make an appointment to see him. He made history in 1977 by being the first Sheriff ever to be dismissed from office, the ostensible reason being that he had engaged in political activity. Along with many others I felt that this was unfair because it required a very liberal interpretation of the words 'political activity', usually taken to imply party political activity. The activity in which he was said to be politically involved was that of the Scottish Plebiscite Society, a body which held local plebiscites on the question of Scotland's constitutional position – whether the status quo should continue or whether Scotland should regain its independence. It was well known that Peter had been running these unofficial little plebiscites for many years, and nobody minded. He maintained that he was not advocating any particular political position, he was simply measuring opinion. But he went too far in attempting to run a plebiscite in Rutherglen where voters were asked to send their votes to 'The Returning Officer, Hamilton Sheriff Court'. This could certainly be read as implying that it was an official matter, for at that time the Sheriffs were the returning officers at Parliamentary elections. So it was not altogether surprising that the Lord President requested him to appear before him to give an account of himself. Peter, alas, was thrawn, and refused to appear. As a result his dismissal had to come about, but it appeared that it was really for being rude to the Lord President as opposed to engaging in political activity. For some years afterwards he maintained his Plebiscite Society, always advocating that all sides of questions should be heard before decisions were made; and when at last the first official referendum on Scotland's future took place in 1979 he appeared on the streets of Glasgow as a rather forlorn self-appointed ombudsman to see that it was conducted fairly.

Training for Sheriffs

It is difficult now to believe, but Sheriffs were expected to start work without any specific training for the job. Most Sheriffs were appointed from the Bar, and while most would have experience of civil debates and proofs in the Sheriff Court, which differed little from those in the Court of Session, and would also have experience of summary criminal trials, few would have been involved in the procedural hearings which led up to either form of work. So, you were one day an advocate, and the next day a Sheriff, without any real knowledge of what was expected of you.

In one of the first cases I presided over I was told that I would have to place someone on probation. How on earth did you do this? I had never seen anyone placed on probation before. My criminal experience had been largely in the High Court, and there people were not placed on probation. None of those clients whom I had unsuccessfully defended as an advocate had ever been made the subject of a probation order – they had all been sent to prison. There was nothing in the textbooks on procedure to indicate what had to be said or done, and it was embarrassing having to consult the sheriff clerk, not only about probation, but also about a host of other things which a Sheriff should know about, but had never been taught. 'Learning by experience' was what was expected, but even in a busy court I believe it would take about two years' experience before a newly appointed Sheriff would feel thoroughly conversant with all that went on.

So I happily joined in the movement towards the establishment of a training programme for Sheriffs. This was particularly necessary as regards sentencing, which I believe to be the most difficult part of a Sheriff's work. Sentencing in the Sheriff Court was a world away from sentencing in the High Court. Many different types of sentence were available to the Sheriff, while – as a rule – a High Court judge only had to think of what would be the appropriate number of years' imprisonment to impose. Judges in the High Court also did not receive any training. From time to time I spoke and wrote about the desirability of judicial training, but was once rather taken aback to find the headline 'Untrained judges think of a number' above a newspaper report of a talk I had given on the subject!

Here England showed the way to Scotland. Despite resistance from many judges, who thought it demeaning to expect them to submit to training (for they believed that they knew it all or could teach themselves), there was eventually established a training course for English judges, both in the High Court and the lower courts, under the direction of what was called – perhaps to spare the feelings of the die-hard old guard – the 'Judicial Studies Board', and all newly appointed judges were required to attend.

It was only in 1996 that formal training under a similar system for High Court judges in Scotland was established. Sheriffs, however, had received training since the 1980s, spending three or four days at a residential course, and sitting for a week in court with an experienced Sheriff. I always found it enjoyable to have a trainee Sheriff sitting with me, since it became a learning experience for me as well as for the trainee. Not only does one learn by teaching, as a general principle, but my explaining to the trainee why I had done what I had done in the cases we heard together was also a valuable exercise in shaking me out of the complacency of routine. In trying to justify my decisions to the trainee I had to try to justify to myself what I had done.

Summary criminal trials

Three-quarters of the work in Hamilton was criminal, and three-quarters of that work was summary trials. I kept statistics for seven years until I found that, year in year out, I had been convicting 75 per cent of those I had tried while sitting by myself. Indeed, if a solicitor had been asked by his client, on hearing that it would be me who would try him, what his chances were of being acquitted, he could accurately have forecast 'one in four'. But this was just in Hamilton. When I sat in Airdrie my conviction rate was only 66 per cent. Since I was the constant factor, the variables had to be the fiscals and the cases which they chose to prosecute. It was thought that in Airdrie the fiscal was 'empire-building', seeking to show what a large volume of work he had to get through, and so cases where the prospects of success were limited would nevertheless be prosecuted in the interests of the figures on the returns of work done. Hamilton, however, had an excellent team of fiscals who only prosecuted, or continued with a prosecution, when the prospects of a successful conviction were good.

The best defence lawyer that I came across in the West was Ian Muirhead of Coatbridge. In appearance he often reminded me of an artist's impression I once saw in *Punch* of a deep depression leaving Iceland. But if he was in fact depressed it might well have been on account of his having taken on far too much work. Such was his ability that he was always in demand and difficult to pin down. There was thought to be a presumption that he would not turn up at court on any date fixed for trial of one of his clients; or, if he did turn up on the right date, there was an almost irrebuttable presumption that he would be late. But when at last he did turn up and got going with his defence, he was extraordinarily good value. Laurence Dowdall, suave and smooth, and Joe Beltrami, hard and unsmiling, were in their different ways the two other criminal practitioners who came into this class in the West. All three had in common a courtesy towards the Bench while presenting a well-prepared, often ingenious and usually rigorous defence for their clients.

Criminal Legal Aid

The defence of the vast majority of persons appearing for trial on criminal charges was conducted under the criminal legal aid scheme whereby the cost of the defence was paid for out of public funds. Unlike civil legal aid, criminal legal aid was granted without any financial contribution being required from the recipient. But whether or not it was granted depended on the Sheriff. There were two tests to be met. One was whether it was in the interests of justice that legal aid be granted, and the other was whether the applicant could meet the costs of his defence without undue hardship. Neither of these tests was satisfactory. The statute gave no guidance as to what was meant by 'the interests of justice'. Many a time I attended meetings of the Western Sheriffs when the question of what the interests of justice might be was discussed, but as Omar Khayyam found in relation to another puzzling question, 'Evermore by that same door as in I went came out.'

In Hamilton all applicants had to appear in person before the Sheriff. I thought that the best way to interpret the 'interests of justice' aspect was to enquire what the nature of the defence was, essentially to see whether it was frivolous or not. But when asked 'What is your defence to the charge?', the applicant would commonly just reply 'Not Guilty'. 'Yes,' I would say, 'but why do you say you are not guilty? Is it because you say you were somewhere else at the time or because you say that someone else committed the crime?' Often enough this did not lead anywhere, as the applicant had not really thought what his defence was (usually because he knew he had no defence), although 'the police are telling lies' would have been perfectly acceptable at that stage as a statement of defence.

But if applicants could seldom say what their defence was, they could never say what the cost of their defence was likely to be – and so the question of whether they could afford to meet that cost without undue hardship could never be answered. Applicants did not ask their solicitors about this. Of course, if asked, their solicitors would probably have replied that it was impossible to say, since there were so many uncertain factors. But when I enquired of one solicitor what estimate of the cost of a trial he would give to a client *not* seeking legal aid, the solicitor replied that he would never dream of charging a private client what he knew he could get from legal aid. In practice, however, most applications were granted – if only because most persons who appeared on common law charges were unemployed, and thus had no money to spend on solicitor's fees.

After a case was finished, the solicitor could apply to the Sheriff under Sec 13(3) of the Legal Aid (Scotland) (Fees in

Criminal Proceedings) Regulations 1984 to certify that the case had been of exceptional length, complexity or difficulty such as to entitle him to a higher fee than normal. It was the Law Society of Scotland – the statutory body to which all practising solicitors have to belong – which originally administered the criminal legal aid scheme, and the Law Society which originally decided whether a case fell within any of these three categories. The cost of criminal legal aid has always been enormous, and when questions were in due course raised about this aspect of the matter, it turned out that most cases had been found to be of exceptional length, complexity or difficulty! So it was then provided that no longer would the Law Society decide whether or not a higher fee was appropriate; this would fall to the Sheriff who had heard the case (a provision described by a leading Glasgow solicitor as 'evil legislation'!). It was distasteful enough for a Sheriff having to decide whether or not to grant legal aid in the first place; it was even more distasteful to decide whether to certify the case as having been exceptionally long, complex or difficult.

One way or another, a great deal of public money went in to criminal legal aid. Applications for it were made on a green coloured form. Some solicitors accordingly referred to criminal legal aid as 'green gold' and I once heard a disillusioned colleague refer, in his cups, to the 'usual bunch of rentamob solicitors sheltering under the green umbrella'. I showed a draft of a paper I had written on the matter to a senior sheriff clerk. It began, 'I believe that a great deal of public money is wasted on criminal legal aid.' She returned it, saying, 'If I were writing this, Sheriff, I would replace "I believe" with "I know".' Eventually I wrote a song about it:–

> *In the bad old days of summary crime*
> *Agents for the poor had a pretty thin time.*
> *They didn't get fat, they didn't get rich*
> *Defending their clients to the very last ditch.*
> *Yes, 'crime doesn't pay' they used to say,*
> *But whoever says the same today?*
> *For a glorious change at last was made,*
> *And along came Criminal Legal Aid!*
>
> *Legal Aid! It's tailor-made*
> *For the poverty-stricken,*

Their heart-beats will quicken
When they get a powerful plea for free!

Legal Aid! Your fees are paid
By HM Exchequer;
Nothing could be better
Than that green form nominating you, that's true!
The fees are fat and the work is minimal,
Hoorah for Criminal Legal Aid!

Legal Aid! Don't be afraid
Of undue hardship –
You'll find that his Lordship
Will grant you a share of the cake, for pity's sake!

Legal Aid! The way that it's played
In the interests of justice
Makes it a must; it's
A mutual benefit scheme, it's a dream!
For the time and the lime it's sublime, it's subliminal!
Hoorah for Criminal Legal Aid!

The trials may be long and complex, they may be quite
difficult too.
But if so, all the better! There's a bonus scheme for you!
And if they are short and simple, or even if they all should
fold,
No matter! Hallelujah! There's no end to that green gold!

Legal Aid! It's known in the trade
That a nice 13(3)
Means a much higher fee!
(In the public service that you give, you've got to live!)

Legal Aid! You make the grade,
And the crooks get it gratis,
It's all very satis –
: factory doing your duty this way, today!
So sing a loud hymn from your holiest hymnal –
Praise be to Criminal –
Unfailing Criminal –
Hoorah for Criminal Legal Aid!

Parliamentary elections

Until the reform of local government in 1975, the duty of supervising parliamentary elections fell upon the Sheriff Court. The Sheriffs acted as the returning officers, the sheriff clerks organized the polling places and recruited the vote-counters from their own staffs and bank tellers. It was a pleasant duty to perform if only in that on polling day you had a day off from your normal work and received a fee for what you did during the day. What you did was to spend much of the day going round the polling places, which were mostly at local authority schools, to see that everything was being done properly and in order. What an eye-opener it was to see inside some of these schools! Although all were run by the same authority, there was a remarkable difference in tone and atmosphere. Some were bright and attractive, the walls hung with lively artwork and posters, the whole place suggesting confidence and progress; others were drab and dull, and gave a general impression of defeat and despair. Since the tone of organizations tends to reflect the persons at the top, I presumed that whatever other factors might be involved in creating these differences, the principal factor must be the different personalities of the different headteachers.

When counting was under way, the returning officer spent the evening chatting to the candidates and their agents, keeping a general eye on the counting, and in particular adjudicating on whether voting papers were spoiled or not. When papers were passed up by the counters for adjudication, you gathered the candidates or their agents together, and asked them for their views as to whether the vote could be accepted or not. Papers containing no crosses against any candidates' names (as often happened) or only the words 'Kick the Pope' scrawled across them (as also often happened) did not present any difficulty: and only on those rare cases where there was disagreement would the Sheriff have to make a decision one way or the other.

The only thing that troubled me was wondering what to do in the event of a tie, despite several recounts. The Act provides that in the event of a tie lots shall be drawn to determine the winner, but it does not prescribe in what manner lots are to be drawn, be it long or short straws, the toss of a coin, or cutting a deck of playing cards …? What might be the odds, I wonder, against the theoretical possibility of the whole House of Commons membership taking their places on the toss of a coin! No lots required to be drawn, however, on the occasion of the first election I attended as assistant to the returning officer, the famous Hamilton by-election of 1967 when Winnie Ewing won the seat with a majority of 1797, thereby starting the SNP bandwagon rolling towards independence. For quite some time after that, when asked to give talks about Scotland's history or future prospects, I entitled the talks '1797 and a' that'. Unlike in the year 1066 nothing memorable happened in the year 1797, but 1797 may otherwise turn out to have been a memorable number.

The Social Work (Scotland) Act 1968

It was while I was at Hamilton that the Social Work (Scotland) Act 1968 came into force. This was a major watershed Act, but I will mention only two features, one good, one not so good. The unquestionably good feature was the introduction of what were called Children's Hearings to deal with children in need of compulsory measures of care. Most of the cases they dealt with arose from children being badly looked after by their parents, while the rest arose from children committing crimes.

Where a child committed a crime, he had previously been brought before the Sheriff's Juvenile Court, and where that child pleaded guilty there would often enough be simply a ten-minute appearance before the Sheriff, with a plea-in-mitigation from the erring child's solicitor being the Sheriff's only help in deciding what to do with him. Under the 1968 Act, however, the Sheriff no longer had to decide what to do with the child: instead of a ten-minute formal appearance in court, the child now sat at a table with his parents, his social worker if he had one, the Reporter, whose public office required him to bring erring or uncared-for children before a Hearing, and the three members of the Children's Hearing itself. All discussed the facts of the matter for up to an hour, and it was an article of faith that it was more likely that an appropriate decision as to the child's future would be reached after an extensive round-table discussion by all the interested parties than by a brief appearance before a single Sheriff.

The downside of the 1968 Act was the disappearance of the probation service. Taking the place of the probation officer – and the place of many other specialized local authority officers – was the generic social worker, expected to be all things to all men. As far as the Sheriffs were concerned this was generally felt to be a disaster. The probation officers had been very familiar figures. There they were in court day-in-day-out, a small number of caring persons whom you got to know well, whose reports you could rely upon, and with whom you could discuss the progress of offenders you had placed on probation. At a stroke they disappeared. Who now wrote the social enquiry report? It came from an unknown hand. Who would supervise the offender you placed on supervision? You had no idea – the supervisor was one of 100 or more social workers unknown to you instead of one of the half-dozen familiar probation officers. Probationers were now in fact attended to by an anonymous and silent service of social workers, and it was hard to tell what was happening by way of supervision other than that there appeared to be an increase in the number of further offences committed by persons ostensibly under supervision. The change in description of those under supervision from probation officers' 'probationers' to social workers' 'clients' summed up the change in attitude. Confidence in probation as a method of dealing with offenders fell off sharply, and during the 1970s and 80s Sheriffs became more likely to defer sentence rather than make what they often began to think was the waste of time of a probation order. It was not until the 1990s that the pendulum swung back. The probation service as such was not, alas, revived, but social workers began to work in specialized fields, of which dealing with offenders was one.

Robes

I once paid a visit to the Crown Court in Durham and asked the doorkeeper which judges were sitting that day. The doorkeeper was an old Scotsman, and replied, 'Aye weel, there's a blue yin, a black yin and a red yin.' By this I understood him to mean that a circuit judge, a Recorder and a High Court judge were sitting, since circuit judges wear blue robes, Recorders wear black robes and High Court judges wear red robes. But Sheriffs do not have a distinctive robe – they are indistinguishable from counsel in simply wearing a black gown. The question of Sheriffs having a distinctive robe to wear has been raised many times over the years, from 1910 onwards, but has never been satisfactorily resolved.

In 1962 the Lord President approved the introduction of a distinctive robe, provided that the Sheriffs Principal agreed. The Sheriffs Principal did not agree, however, and there the matter rests, although it is still revived from time to time. Personally I thought it was absurd that Sheriffs did not have a distinctive robe, and were indeed the only order of judges in a royal court to be in this position. It seemed to me that while Sheriffs would be pleased and proud to wear special robes if such robes arrived in their chambers without asking, they nevertheless did not want to ask for them and make them arrive for fear of attracting ridicule. Very well then. Assuming that the asking for robes is ridiculous, but that Sheriffs do ask for them, what would happen? There would no doubt be cheerful third leaders in the *Scotsman* and the *Herald*, *Private Eye* might even have a giggle, and Cameron Miller would certainly rewrite the spiritual 'I gotta robe, you gotta robe, all God's chillun got robes'. Then, the ridicule over, Sheriffs would settle down to wear what I hope they will indeed in due course wear, a robe suitably befitting their dignity as an independent order of judges.

Motherwell v Hearts

One of the problems affecting the diary at Hamilton Sheriff Court was the fact that Fir Park, the ground of the Motherwell football team, was within the Sheriff Court's jurisdiction and that Motherwell had regular games there against the Edinburgh team Hearts. For some reason (never satisfactorily explained to me), there was a peculiar needle between supporters of Motherwell and supporters of Hearts, so much so that normally a week would have to be set aside for the breach of the peace trials that inevitably followed. I attended the matches once or twice to see at first hand what they were like, and my abiding memory is of the police establishing a passageway between the rival sets of supporters on the terracing and patrolling this *cordon sanitaire* with dogs. The Hearts supporters bayed at the Motherwell supporters, the Motherwell supporters bayed at the Hearts supporters, and the police dogs bayed at both. All were united, however, in baying at the referee, with whom, as a fellow judge of first instance, I had much sympathy.

Farewell to the West

Upon my appointment as Sheriff at Hamilton it had been necessary to choose somewhere in Lanarkshire to live, and without much difficulty my wife and I settled for Strathaven, just a few miles from Hamilton and probably the most attractive little town in the whole county. After ten years I applied to be transferred to Edinburgh, primarily in the interests of the education of our two children, Ingalo and Diggi. They had been at a parents' do-it-yourself co-operative private school; it had met in the drawing-room of a house in Strathaven and had only ten children on the roll. Such individual attention had been a marvellous start to their schooling, but they now required a broader educational canvas.

I had become greatly attached to Hamilton Sheriff Court and its excellent family of solicitors, fiscals, clerks and court officers, so although I was glad when my request to be transferred was granted, I was sorry to leave Hamilton, Strathaven and the West in general. I knew that as an Edinburgh man I was supposed to disapprove of all things western, but I had come to enjoy Lanarkshire greatly, and to this day, every time I meet someone from Hamilton Sheriff Court or someone with a Glasgow accent my heart sings a little, for I know that I will have met a cheery and a friendly person.

4

Strathaven Arts Guild

The Arts in Scotland

In the 1960s Strathaven was still at heart a sleepy little market town, preserving the homely virtues of rural Lanarkshire and anxious to distinguish between natives and incomers. But physically, it was a particularly attractive town, with many old wynds and closes, a picturesque 'village square', a ruined castle, a beautiful golf course and a public park of the first quality.

What it did not have, however, was much of an artistic life. This was not surprising, because the tradition of Scotland being a hard man's land was still strong. At the end of World War II Scotland held two unenviable positions in international league tables. It was top of the European prison-population-in-proportion-to-total-population league, and it was bottom of the European artistic participation league. Whether there was any connection between these two positions is not certain, but what can be said is that graciousness of expression, through whatever medium, was not highly regarded as a national virtue.

Scotland's creative energies during the previous two or three centuries had, of course, been formidable. Engineering, theology and medicine were only a few of the channels into which they had been poured and from which they had brought forth widely acclaimed triumphs. But somehow the arts had missed out. With the exception of two or three writers, painters and architects, no Scotsman had achieved international, much less world-class, standing in the arts. Physicists, soldiers, politicians, explorers – yes, Scotland had produced these aplenty: but composers, playwrights, dancers, sculptors – of these Scotland had next to none.

After the war, however, the scene was greatly changed. The Edinburgh International Festival arrived. The Scottish National Orchestra was re-formed. Scottish Opera was born. Slowly the world outside began to realize that Scotland was not a cultural desert, and that, at least in its larger cities, it was possible to find an internationally acceptable level of artistic life.

Outside of the cities, however, there was little change. Professional performers were seldom seen, and although amateur groups of all sorts flourished, they did so despite, or – so the cynic might say – because of an almost invincible repugnance for seeking quality in their performances. But change there began to be. The Scottish Arts Council looked beyond the cities, and formulated a policy for promoting the arts in the landward areas by subsidizing the cost of presenting professionals to local audiences in their local halls. The Arts Council did not engage or present them directly, but they encouraged the formation of music clubs and arts guilds up and down the land, and left it to these local bodies to choose and present their own programmes. This was a bold and imaginative policy. When properly applied, it meant that local people could enjoy top-class professional artistes without having to travel to Glasgow or Edinburgh and without having to pay Edinburgh and Glasgow prices.

The Arts in Strathaven

Could this be applied in Strathaven? Well, a Stravonian called Bob Currie thought it could. He was a young man of immense vision and energy; interested in both music and drama, and having started a family, he wanted his children to grow up in an atmosphere where participation in the arts would be looked upon as a normal and natural part of everyday life. So he set about knocking on doors, decided there was a sufficient level of support to call a public meeting on the matter, and persuaded me to become chairman of the Arts Guild which the meeting resolved to establish.

We started with a home-made entertainment of song and laughter, the performers coming from organizations already existing or just starting – Rotary, Round Table, the Churches, the Male-Voice choir and the Recorder Ensemble. Amateurs all, of course, and the Guild committee were determined to keep the needs, talents and the infinite potential of local amateurs always before them. The committee also determined that amateurs and professionals must be looked upon as complementary. Professionals require a flourishing amateur world as the heartland of their audiences; and amateurs require professionals in their midst to set standards continuously before them.

So the next show was professional. Standards were set for us in verse speaking, tenor song and piano playing; and during the first year of the Guild's life the King's Singers sang in Strathaven, Scottish Theatre Ballet danced in Strathaven, Emilio Coia sketched in Strathaven, and in Strathaven the broadcaster Antony Hopkins talked about music. The local amateurs responded impressively, and various groups were assisted into being by the Guild – a drama group which took the name of the Aven Players, a Film Club, the Strathaven and District Pipe Band, and the Strathaven Corps of Drum Majorettes. The jewel in the Arts Guild's crown, however, was Strathaven Choral Society, which soon belonged in the front rank of choral societies in Scotland.

It was at first difficult to realize that all this was actually happening, and in particular that public money from local and national authorities was coming into Strathaven to support the arts, so that for no more than the price of a cinema ticket people in Strathaven could see, hear and appreciate for themselves the quality and standards which only professionals of the first order could provide by personal appearances in Strathaven. If Scotland had once been a hard man's land, fit for philistines to live in, this was a Scotland of which Strathaven had ceased to form part. Bob Currie's idea was being realized, and thanks to his enterprise and vision, the arts were gradually coming to be recognized as something normal and natural in everyday life in Strathaven.

One of the first things which the Guild committee had done was to consider the question of premises in which its activities could take place. There were only two available properties in the town which might be suitable for conversion into an arts centre. Both, however, presented formidable problems, and nothing else appeared to be suitable or likely to come on to the market. *Faute de mieux* the shows continued to be presented chiefly in the all-purpose community centre, the Balgreen Hall, which resembled nothing so much as an outsize shoebox. Its only stage facility was a curtain; its tubular chairs sat on a flat floor; it had no atmosphere at all.

The East Church scheme

Then an idea occurred to me. I had become a member of Strathaven's East Church, where one of my great-great-grandfathers, John French, had been the minister in the 1820s. The church building was capable of holding almost 800, 500 in the downstairs pews and 300 in the raked gallery, which was built on three sides of the square building. It seemed to me that a floor could be constructed to infill the well contained by the three sides of the gallery, and that an upstairs auditorium with 300 tiered seats could thereby be created to serve the dual purpose of being used for church services on Sundays, and for concerts and plays on other days of the week. The downstairs area could then be reconstructed to provide meeting rooms for church and community purposes, and the hall in the basement could even be used as a community restaurant. The essence of the scheme was that without prejudice to it being used as a church on Sundays, the East Church would be used as an arts centre on the other days of the week.

I saw this scheme as likely to benefit both the Church and the Guild. From the Church's point of view it would mean a modernization of its ageing interior, a sharing of the cost of future maintenance and, most of all, a visible demonstration of the Church's concern for the parish it served, for the main part of the building was used for only two hours per week – otherwise it lay empty and, literally, useless. Here was a means of giving it a useful life for the benefit of the community for many more than two hours per week. Further, the Church's bicentenary in 1977 was not far off, and the scheme could be a spectacular way of marking the occasion. The proposed dramatic alteration of the fabric of the building might lead to an equally dramatic improvement of the role of the Church in the life of the town – pointing towards the twenty-first century instead of back to the eighteenth century, from which one sometimes thought it had never really wanted to emerge. The scheme was in effect an extension of what had become the accepted concept of the 'congregational hall/church' into that of a 'community theatre/church'.

From the Guild's point of view it would mean that a building would be available which could provide suitable accommodation for all its needs. The major objective of an auditorium with tiered seating for up to 300 would be achieved, and rooms for small group meetings and activities would be created. Further, the capital and revenue costs would be shared.

While there would be these manifest advantages for both bodies, there would also be difficulties and problems. Perhaps the main disadvantage of such a scheme was the possibility of friction, which is not unknown to occur when accommodation is shared. The natives–incomers tension might be heightened, for the Church membership was largely native and the Arts Guild members were mostly incomers. Further, the formal relationship between the Church and the Guild would be that of landlord and tenant; and among the pieces of advice which Polonius might have given to Laertes was 'Neither a landlord nor a tenant be'. The Kirk Session, however, did not reject the scheme in principle when it was first put to them. Encouraged to this extent, I proceeded to make a wooden model to demonstrate what the East Church building could look like if transformed into a community theatre/ church, and after hearing further explanation of the scheme with the assistance of the model, the Kirk Session gave permission to the Arts Guild to carry out a feasibility study.

The Guild on television

It so happened that one of my brothers-in-law was the well-known broadcaster Magnus Magnusson. I showed the model to a family gathering at Christmas 1972. Magnus saw the visual possibilities of the model and the controversial principle it embodied, and suggested building a television programme round it. Not surprisingly this suggestion was taken up, and in due course Magnus with his producer, director and camera crew came to Strathaven. They filmed inside the East Church, and they filmed, literally, inside the model. They examined many aspects of the Guild's activities to see what best might feature in the programmes, and they engendered a high sense of excitement among the Choral Society and the Recorder Ensemble who were asked to go to the studio in Glasgow for their part in the composite programme, scheduled for 25th March 1973.

This turn of events was as unexpected as it was dramatic. Welcome as the nationwide publicity would be for the Guild and its accommodation problems, there was the immediate problem of publicity for the scheme in Strathaven itself in advance of the broadcast. For although the Kirk Session was familiar with the scheme, the congregation as a whole knew nothing of it officially, and it clearly would not help the prospects of the scheme if members of the congregation were to switch on their television sets and without warning see their church building being turned into a theatre before their very eyes. So a local press conference was called, and the scribes of the *Strathaven and Stonehouse News*, the *Hamilton Advertiser* and the *East Kilbride News* were given the full story. One of them caused considerable damage to the prospects of the scheme by printing as a front-page banner headline 'Theatre-Kirk but never on a Sunday'. The sleazy implication of this was not lost: God's house might be in danger of becoming a whores' house – a description often given to the theatre 200 years ago. Double distress was thus suffered by those members of the East Church who preferred to stay with the eighteenth century rather than look forward to the twenty-first. Not only might incomers be taking over their church building, but they might be doing so for eventually immoral purposes! As one elder put it, the threat of Reds-under-the-beds was nothing as to the threat of the Arts Guild in the East Church.

Despite this unfortunate advance publicity, the television show went well. The Choral Society gave a spirited rendering of the 'Gloria' from Haydn's *St Theresa Mass*, the Recorder Ensemble produced both the elegant melancholy of a seventeenth-century pavane and the knockabout fun of a twentieth-century hoedown, and clips were shown of various other Guild organizations in action. I sang a Tom Lehrer song and a Danny Kaye song at the piano and demonstrated the possibilities of the Theatre-Church with the model. Magnus put searching questions to the studio audience about the Guild, and equally searching questions about the East Church scheme to the ministers of the three Strathaven churches in the audience. Two of them welcomed the scheme in principle, and the third, the minister of the East Church itself, discreetly confined himself to reporting on the generally adverse reaction from his congregation. Generally adverse, too, was reaction to the show in the town at large. One perceptive native put it this way: 'The trouble with the show was that in it the Guild excelled, and in Strathaven you are not supposed to excel.'

The end of the East Church scheme

The aftermath of the television show was brisk and business-like. Special meetings of the Kirk Session and of the congregation were called, and these might well have made exciting television shows themselves! Clearly there was support for the scheme in the congregation, but it was muted. Very clearly there was opposition to the scheme, and it was vociferous. One member was 'Totally, wholly and utterly opposed to it'; another proclaimed that if the scheme went through, he would withdraw from the congregation 'himself and his wife and children' – and it almost sounded as if he were going to add 'his manservant and his maidservant, his ox, yea, his ass'.

I had no wish to split the congregation and had forborne to lobby on the matter. Eventually, however, I moved, as an elder of the congregation, that the scheme be approved. This was followed by silence. The minister Hector Steele – whose conduct throughout a very trying six months' controversy had been exemplary – then said that inasmuch as the motion had failed to find a seconder, he declared it to be lost. This was greeted with loud and general applause. He then added, 'At the same time a vote of thanks should be afforded to Sheriff Thomson for the time and trouble he has spent on the matter.' This was followed by faint and scattered applause; and there ended the East Church scheme.

The Old Town Hall scheme

The next scheme on which we embarked was an attempt to acquire the Old Town Hall. For many years it had served as a cinema, and all along it had served as a dance hall. Many a Strathaven couple had indeed first met at 'the dancing' in the Old Town Hall. But after World War II the demand for public dancing dwindled; keeping the hall open became uneconomic; and it effectively closed down in the early 1960s. When the Guild committee had first looked at it, the burden of restoring and maintaining it had seemed to be insuperable; but after the East Church scheme had failed, the Guild committee began to think again about the Old Town Hall, heartened by the growing strength of the Guild and by indications that there might be support from public funds.

Two other parties, however, had also begun to think about the Old Town Hall. One was the Scouts and Guides, who, like the Guild, also lacked adequate premises for their activities. The other was a former Rangers footballer, Eric Caldow, who wanted to turn the hall into what was described as a 'social club'. The Guild and the Scouts and Guides at first considered the possibility of jointly using the hall, but came to the conclusion that this would be impracticable, and each then devised plans for its exclusive use.

Which of the three interested parties would succeed in acquiring the hall? This question was lovingly canvassed by the local press, who ran the story for weeks. The Guild believed it had to offer substantially more than its rivals, for the directors of the company that owned the hall were not thought to be artistically inclined, and had indeed in their time had an interest in the Scouts. Finding an appropriate figure to offer, however, was a perplexing task. It was difficult enough for a surveyor to put a value on such an unusual building. The Guild's task was made easier, however, by Lanark County Council intimating, with remarkable speed, that it was prepared to make a grant of £10,000 to the Guild for purchasing the hall.

The day at last came when offers were opened. Mr Caldow's offer was less than £12,000. The Scouts and Guides had offered £12,000. And the Guild had offered £12,000. Other things being equal, the Scouts and Guides were likely to get the hall: and as other things were equal, they did. 'Victory for Youth' was the headline in the local press; and there ended the Old Town Hall scheme.

The Town Mill scheme

Played two, lost two. Undismayed, the Guild now looked at a number of other properties, but found them all to be unavailable or unsuitable. And then, in January 1974, I was invited to have a look at the ruined Town Mill.

Although I had lived in Strathaven at that time for over seven years, this was the first time I had ever seen its venerable mill. On the main road there was what appeared to be a one-floor brick-built building adjacent to a roofless ruin, which in turn adjoined an imposing doorway with the words 'The Town Mill' and 'For quality better canna be' carved upon it; but to the passer-by on wheels there was nothing to suggest that there was anything more. Unless you knew where to look, you would never see the Mill. If you stopped and looked closely, however, you would see that such was the steep fall of the land that there were three floors below the street-level buildings, and that these four-floored buildings, collectively forming the Granary, were connected by a bridge to another four-floored building, the Mill proper.

Both buildings were in an advanced state of decay, however, and only the walls appeared to be sound. The Mill had been built in the early seventeenth century, but had been empty since 1966 when production ceased. The Granary had been gutted by a blaze in 1970, and in 1972 the Mill's roof had collapsed: old age and the weather had combined with fire to make both buildings derelict. Nor was the Mill made any more attractive by a large iron-roofed shed which had been propped against its front facade in 1920, or by the jungle of vegetation which had grown up against its back. A *Glasgow Herald* journalist put it this way: 'The place is a cavernous ruin. So far as it shows signs of recent occupation, it can only have been by Dracula in a bad mood.'

It was a damp, dull day when I first went to look at it. But the warmth of the owner's welcome, her belief that something might be done with these buildings similar to what she had seen done by the Dowager Duchess of Hamilton with the old mill in Haddington, and the realization that these buildings were extensive, were there at all and were available – all this removed a good deal of the dullness and the dampness from the day. Encouraged by what I had seen, I called in the Guild's Director of Works, John Vince, who, similarly encouraged, called in a local architect, John Gray. The Granary seemed to be the likelier of the two buildings to be capable of restoration, and – to my everlasting disgrace – the first question I actually put to the architect was 'How much do you think it would cost to demolish the Mill?'

John Gray was made of sterner stuff, however. Yes, he said, it was possible to restore both Mill and Granary and transform them into an arts centre. It would take a great deal of sustained effort and enthusiasm and a great deal of money, but it could be done. This was enough for the Guild committee, and I was instructed to give a very simple two-word instruction to the Director of Works and the architect. They were the words once used by Diaghilev to Cocteau on commissioning a new ballet, simply, 'Étonnez-moi!'

But neither of them would be able to do anything astonishing if there was nothing to work on. The Mill was perilously near to passing beyond recall; and so an emergency programme of first-aid to its structure had to be undertaken at once. At the beginning of February 1974, volunteers from the Guild moved in, treading delicately on rotting timbers, bypassing piles of rubble, sliding over slates, and, roped together, catwalking on what remained of the roof. It was certainly a fitting set for a horror picture, and I did indeed write to Hammer Films asking if they would be interested in it – for rusty chains were here and there to be found, nooses of rope hung from some of the rafters, and the brick-built drying kiln, shaped like a monstrous funnel and extending to the height of three floors, might well have been the *oubliette* of a medieval castle. It would have been so simple to push a forgettable person into the sinister yawn of that funnel …

At any rate, these Dracula-defying volunteers worked away every Saturday morning, anxious to get at least a makeshift roof up as soon as possible. After several weeks the rafters were at last in position, sarking was nailed into place, and tarpaulins were slung over it. This was a considerable achievement. Not only did it save the building from further gross penetration by the weather, and start its drying out, but it demonstrated convincingly what could be done with the sustained application of enthusiastic volunteers. The public – both within and outwith Strathaven – had to be convinced that the Guild was in earnest about this project; and here was very real evidence of its intentions.

This first-aid work was an act of faith. It might all be wasted effort if the cost of the intensive care required was going to be beyond the bounds of possibility. Now the French have at least two words for the bill at the end of a meal – not just *l'addition*, but *la douleureuse*, and here the sadness of the bill was estimated to add up to £100,000 at 1974 prices, which was roughly £100,000 more than the Guild had in its bank account. But the sadness was not unrelieved. Had not the County Council rallied round, and quickly too, with a promise of £10,000 for the abortive Town Hall project? Were there not now 400 members in the Guild? And was not the project flexible, in that parts of it could be completed and still yield a worthwhile arts centre although the project in its entirety might be beyond attainment? These three considerations impelled the committee to set up the Town Mill campaign.

The Town Mill campaign

The campaign was designed to operate both within Strathaven and further afield. The first thing to do was to secure patrons. There was no difficulty whatsoever in deciding whom to approach as principal patron. Since the Mill had been built under the auspices of the second Duke of Hamilton, it was obviously appropriate that, thirteen Dukes later, his descendant should be behind its rebuilding. His Grace readily consented to be the patron-in-chief, and thereafter twelve other patrons were secured, six of high local standing and six of high national standing. These included Lord Clydesmuir, the Lord Lieutenant of Lanarkshire, Sir Andrew Gilchrist, Ambassador emeritus, who, no doubt on the principle of *bis dat qui cito dat* (he gives twice who gives quickly), made the very first contribution of cash to the campaign, Sir Alexander Gibson, conductor of the Scottish National Orchestra, Sir William MacTaggart, past president of the Royal Scottish Academy, Nicol Williamson the actor, Angus MacVicar the writer, Una McLean, doyenne of Scottish comediennes, herself a Stravonian, and, not surprisingly, Magnus Magnusson.

'And wha could refuse the laird wi' a' that?' With this impressive list of patrons to refer to, the task of assembling a campaign committee was made much less difficult, though it took me out knocking on doors night after night for a month non-stop. But with a project of such magnitude it was obviously necessary to gain the support of the Guild as a whole, especially since it was known that there were faint hearts and doubting Thomases. But with planning permission and a firm option to purchase obtained, with costs agreed with the County Council, and with a complete order of battle assembled by way of patrons and campaign committee, the Guild committee could now with some confidence call an extraordinary general meeting of the Guild with a view to the Guild as a whole authorizing the project. When this took place, Thomases voiced their doubts, and hearts inclined to faint duly fainted; but by a large majority the Guild decided to proceed with the purchase of the property and to instruct the campaign committee to enter the field.

Off went collectors to every door in Strathaven. Off went letters by the dozen appealing to charitable trusts and industrial companies. And on went the work of amassing what amounted to a volunteer labour force of eighty, who were clearly capable of carrying out several thousand pounds worth of work. In the initial stages it was, of course, people who could handle saws and hammers or mix sand and cement who had much to occupy them; and picks, shovels and wheelbarrows were still at work each Saturday morning, still removing the debris in the Mill and the *matto grosso* of overgrown vegetation around it. But how to co-ordinate the work of volunteers and that of the specialist contractors who would be required? And in the event of an accident what would the Guild's position be? To resolve these difficulties the Guild committee decided to form a limited company of its own to act as main contractors on the project. Mill Restorations Ltd was accordingly incorporated, with a share capital of £100, of which only two shares were ever issued. While this meant that suppliers might think twice about supplying goods to the company – until they realized that the private and public funds to be raised by the Guild were behind it – it also meant that liability in the event of an accident would be limited. The Guild committee then leased the whole buildings to the company. In the event of an accident, liability for any negligence would attach to the occupier. The Guild was the owner, but Mill Restorations Ltd was the occupier.

John Vince, our Director of Works, was another young man of immense vision and energy. He was managing director of his own light engineering company, and as a keen member of the Arts Guild, was happy to become managing director of Mill Restorations Ltd also, and to make office and workshop space available to the new company in his own company's premises.

There was just one difficulty, however, in Mill Restorations getting to work. The Guild had spent all the money it had so far raised on the materials involved in its first-aid work on the buildings, in the purchase of the property and in the cost of forming the company. The Guild had nothing it could then give the company to work with, and with only two pounds of share capital to play with, Mill Restorations Ltd simply had to mark time and wait, like Mr Micawber, for something to turn up.

Money pours in

It never rains but it pours; and in Strathaven Mr Micawber had to rush for his umbrella. A perfectly respectable but inevitably modest amount was raised from the appeal to private funds, personal and corporate. The appeal to public funds, on the other hand, was so successful that eventually the Scottish Office appointed a special investigator to see how Strathaven Arts Guild had received so much from so many parts of the public purse. In these days public money was available in quantities undreamed of today, and it just poured in. East Kilbride District Council put up money. The Scottish Arts Council put up money. The Historic Buildings Council put up money and money also came from that part of the Regional Council which had responsibility for historic buildings of local interest. The Mill stood on a tourist crossroads and with a little persuasion the Scottish Tourist Board put up a goodly sum. Harder to get, however, was money from what we had expected would be our principal benefactors – the education authorities. But eventually they too, at both national and regional level, were persuaded to make over significant sums to the project.

The most significant sums, however, came from the Job Creation Programme. Under this scheme the Manpower Services Commission would meet the costs of creating jobs on work of social benefit where persons who would otherwise be unemployed could be employed. It was a condition of receiving such assistance that the beneficiaries find, employ and administer the otherwise unemployed workers. This was not something which the Guild itself could have done, but of course it now had in being its own company, Mill Restorations Ltd. Appropriately enough, the first person engaged was an out-of-work wages clerkess – to pay the wages of all the out-of-work labourers and tradesmen who were about to find work again, at the Mill, and there were many of them.

When John Vince broke the news to me that our application to the Manpower Services Commission had been successful, and was worth the best part of £100,000 in free labour, my joyful expletives had to be deleted. This was the turning-point, and ensured the successful completion of the project. From then on it was full steam ahead, and the restoration and development of the buildings proceeded steadily. The ground floor of the Mill was transformed into a clubroom, the bar being formed from some of the original mill timbers. The first floor became the technical support area for the theatre, and the second floor became the theatre proper, seating 150 on raked seats rescued from a redundant cinema and installed by prisoners from nearby Dungavel Prison. The theatre was connected by an enclosed bridge to the Granary, which was later developed to comprise a theatre foyer, a function room, an art gallery and a craft workshop.

Curtain up

Attention then shifted to furnishing and equipment. The first major purchase, subsidized by the Arts Council, was a Bechstein boudoir grand piano, which had suffered an unhappy life in a dance hall. Its keys looked as if they had not been to the dentist for years, and the woodwork looked as if a treeful of owls had been using it as a scratching pad – nevertheless, the fact that it was there at all, and, like the Mill, was capable of restoration, made it look entirely beautiful!

In October 1977 the curtain went up on the first professional show in the Town Mill Theatre, the distinguished Scottish actor Leonard Maguire presenting his one-man version of three short stories by Robert Louis Stevenson. Mr Maguire was the first of many professional artistes to remark on the attractive nature of the theatre – its intimacy, its acoustics, and its blend of ancient and modern in its decoration all adding up to provide an unusually pleasant setting for a theatrical experience. It had always been the Guild's policy to present a wide range of artistes, and among those who appeared during the first years of the theatre's life were Lawrence Glover, Jean Redpath, the New Music Group of Scotland, Scottish Ballet Movable Workshop, Paines Plough Theatre, Delphine and Domingo, and Theatre about Glasgow.

This, of course, was just one part of the life of the Town Mill Theatre. Professional and amateur activity had always been regarded as complementary and mutually dependent. By the time the Mill was opened there were a dozen groups associated with the Guild as corporate members; several of the performing groups used the theatre for rehearsal and performance, and other groups used it for straightforward meetings. It housed art classes and classes in guitar and violin. It became a cinema for the Film Society, a drawing room for the Recorder Ensemble, a howff for the Folk Club and a pad for traditional jazz.

These years, from the foundation of Strathaven Arts Guild in 1971 to the completion of the Town Mill Theatre in 1977 were, I think, the 'time of my life'. When I retired as founder-chairman on moving to Edinburgh I was presented with a gavel made from the original timbers of the Mill. Engraved upon it were these words: 'What we call results are but beginnings.' Strathaven Town Mill served the community in one way for its first 300 years. It has now begun to serve it, in another way, for what should be at least another 300 years.

5

Edinburgh Sheriff Court

The Courthouse

The courthouse in the Lawnmarket at the crossroads of the Mound, George IV Bridge and the High Street was built in 1937. It provided courts and accommodation for four Sheriffs; the procurators fiscal were all housed within it; and the building was presumably considered to be large enough to meet all needs for the foreseeable future. After the war, however, with the growth in crime, with the arrival of legal aid from public funds to help meet the cost of civil litigation, and in particular to meet the whole cost of defending criminal cases, there was such an expansion of work that the courthouse became quite unable to meet all the demands being made upon it.

So, one after another, various parts of the work of the Sheriff Court were sent off to other buildings. The fiscals all departed to Queensferry Street. India Buildings at the top of Victoria Street provided two courts for criminal cases, and later on the whole civil department was moved there. Jury trials took place in the Church of Scotland's Assembly Hall. Summary trials took place in hastily converted buildings in Rose Street, in Palmerston Place and in Market Street. The Assembly Hall was replaced by Argyle House as the setting for jury trials, and the civil department eventually moved from India Buildings to Lauriston House. What had originally been contained within one building in the High Street latterly required six different buildings to accommodate it.

The inconvenience of it all was very clear. The fiscals were far away and not readily accessible as they had been for negotiations with defence solicitors. They had to be mini-bussed up to court, and last-minute negotiations frequently led to long delays in the start of trials. Conducting a jury trial in the Assembly Hall was a strange experience. The Sheriff used the Moderator's retiring room, approaching it up a staircase hung with photographs of right reverend gentlemen of past years, a humbling thing to do. In the hall a temporary 'bench' replaced what the Church of Scotland jokingly referred to as the 'playpen' – the wooden-pillared enclosure where former moderators sit during meetings of the General Assembly. On either side of the bench were a temporary jury box and a temporary witness box; the fiscal commonly stood in front of the jury box when examining witnesses, but so far apart from each other were the witness box and jury box that following the cut and thrust of question and answer was like watching a tennis match from the umpire's chair – one's neck became weary of much turning this way, then that way, then this way again and so on. The Assembly Hall seats 1500, and during the Edinburgh Festival it is used for large-scale dramatic productions before packed houses. When used for a jury trial, however, it attracted no audience, and one had the curious feeling of being part of a phantom theatre company waiting for a playwright to come along to put us in a play. And the buildings used for civil work and summary trials all had their drawbacks, if only in that they were a long way from the Lawnmarket motherhouse; this meant endless taxi journeys backwards and forwards and frequent delays to the start of summary trials through people having gone to the wrong building.

A new and comprehensive courthouse was required. This would obviously be a colossal undertaking, and so it proved to be. The site selected was that occupied in Chambers Street by Heriot-Watt University. Normally one thought of the Heriot-Watt as simply being the listed building opposite the museum, but that was a relatively small part of it. Behind and attached to the listed building was a nine-floor brick-built and eminently unlistable building which one never saw unless one knew where to look. It had to be totally demolished. The Sheriffs had assumed, when first told about the move to the Heriot-Watt site, that the listed building would provide an appropriately dignified front facade to the new Sheriff Court, and it came as an unwelcome shock to find that the listed building was to become the new Crown Office – with the new Sheriff Court tagged on to and tucked away behind it, with no front facade at all. It also came as an unwelcome shock to find that it had been decided not to proceed with the proposal to link the new Sheriff Courthouse to the Parliament House complex by a bridge over the Cowgate, which would have made the constant access required by solicitors from the one building to the other so very much easier.

That said, however, I have nothing but praise for the new Sheriff Courthouse, opened in 1995. It was a triumph for the architect and builders. It might be said that its interior resembles an art gallery awaiting the arrival of the sculpture rather than a courthouse awaiting the arrival of the law, and it is fitted out to a very high standard. What a change from 1937! Parking in the basement, restaurants, a gymnasium, showers, computers everywhere. The fiscals were back again under the same roof. Four courtrooms in 1937, sixteen courtrooms now. But for how long, one wonders, will the 1995 building be large enough for all the needs of the Sheriff Court?

Criminal trials

It of course took a little while to adjust to the different tempo of court life in Edinburgh when I moved there in 1976. I had, as it were, to retune from Radio Clyde to Radio Forth. In the civic promotional language of the day, if the Glasgow solicitors had been miles better, the Edinburgh solicitors were slightly superior – or vice versa. The most obvious difference in the work was in criminal appeals. Where an appeal is taken against conviction after a summary trial, the Sheriff has to state a case in writing for the High Court. This takes time, and in so many cases was a waste of time, for many an appeal was abandoned before it could be heard. But in Edinburgh the High Court was just across the road from the Sheriff Court; it was so easy for an Edinburgh solicitor to lodge appeal papers there and to brief counsel. In Hamilton, however, solicitors thought twice before taking an appeal, knowing that they would have to instruct an Edinburgh solicitor to do this for them, and that that would involve them writing at some length about the case to their Edinburgh correspondents. At any rate, I had more appeals taken against my decisions in summary criminal cases in my first year in Edinburgh than in all the ten years I was in Hamilton. Again no doubt because of proximity, many more advocates appeared in the Sheriff Court in Edinburgh than in Hamilton. Of all who appeared before me, incidentally, the one by whom I was the most impressed was a junior counsel called Alan Rodger – who went on to become Lord President of the Court of Session.

Trials could be dull and trials could be fascinating; but the most entertaining trial I ever took part in was in fact a mock trial, staged as a charity fundraiser. I acted as the judge, and an all-star cast of popular solicitors and advocates had been assembled to play the part of witnesses. Dan McKay played the part of the accused, charged with assault and robbery at an Agatha Christie-style house party. The victim was played by the irrepressible Rosie Morrison, who fluttered her eyelashes to great effect in the jury's favour, branding the redoubtable Dan as a double-dyed villain who had sought to take advantage of her. Dan denied everything in the witness box. He discharged verbal blunderbusses in Rosie's disfavour, loudly protested his innocence and stood fast to his special defence of impeachment, by which he incriminated the kenspeckle Donald McNeill McWilliam! I do not remember if there was a conviction, but with these three well-loved lawyers as principals it was all great fun, and given added point by Ludovic Kennedy, who, like Barrington Dalby at broadcast boxing matches, gave inter-round summaries as the trial proceeded.

Of real jury trials over which I presided I remember two as having unusual jury foremen. One was in Jedburgh, where the foreman was the magical dancer of yesteryear, Moira Shearer, Ludovic Kennedy's wife. Such was Ludovic Kennedy's involvement at that time with miscarriages of justice, real or suspected, that it came as no surprise when the verdict was 'not proven'. The other was Sandy Dunbar, the then Director of the Scottish Arts Council, whom I knew quite well. After the jury he was serving on had retired, I had scarcely had time to return to my chambers and take off my wig than in came the court officer to say that the jury was back. They returned a majority guilty verdict, and afterwards I spoke to Sandy and asked him how they had been out for only three minutes. 'Well,' he said, 'they asked me to be foreman and I straightaway asked them for a show of hands. One was for not guilty, two for not proven and the other twelve for guilty – so there wasn't any point in discussing the matter.' So that's what comes from having a professional committee chairman in charge of a jury!

Credo quia impossibile

Much of a Sheriff's time in a trial is occupied with trying to decide whether or not to believe what a witness is saying. Although required to take notes, often enough I put my pen down quite quickly when the accused was giving evidence. I noted the essence of what he had to say, then simply concentrated my full attention on his personal presence in the witness box. Was this an honest man who was speaking? Did he come across as being the clean potato? Was what he was saying too good to be true?

Occasionally, perhaps once every five years, I found myself thinking of applying the approach of a cynical medieval theologian: *credo quia impossibile* – I believe this because it is impossible, it is the very impossibility of this being true which compels me to accept that it *is* true. In other words, stories were occasionally told that appeared to be too good not to be true. One case where I considered that this maxim might just apply was a case of police assault in Dalkeith. A police sergeant gave evidence that he had seen two men behaving suspiciously late one Friday evening. He said that when he had gone up to speak to them one of them took an open razor from his pocket and held it up as if to strike a blow. But he had managed to catch the man's arm and the blow did not land. The man pleaded not guilty, went to trial and gave evidence.

'How,' said the fiscal in cross-examination, 'do you explain having an open razor in your possession?' The accused replied that he always had an open razor to scrape his feet. 'But,' said the fiscal, 'there you were at midnight, downtown in Dalkeith – surely you weren't going to be scraping your feet there and then?' 'No,' said the accused, 'but I was going to be spending the weekend with the friend I was with.' The fiscal decided to test this suggestion that the accused was going off for a weekend. 'So,' he said, 'you were going off for the weekend, were you? Did you have this open razor for shaving with?' 'No,' replied the accused, 'I only use the open razor for scraping my feet; I always use my friend's electric razor for shaving.' 'Well, nevertheless,' said the fiscal, 'you were off for the weekend, and you would no doubt have your weekend kit with you. Did you have a bag or a suitcase with you?' 'No, I didn't need a bag or suitcase.' 'Well, what about your pyjamas? Did you have them with you?' 'Oh no, never wear pyjamas.' 'Did you have your toothbrush with you?' 'No, no, never brush my teeth.' 'So,' said the fiscal, 'do you mean to say that when you go away for the weekend, all you take with you by way of weekend kit is simply an open razor to scrape your feet? Is that what you want the Sheriff to believe?' 'Yes,' he replied. And would you believe it? – I didn't believe him. It had been a good story, but not so impossibly good that I believed it to be true.

Another defence which came near to being too good not to be true – but did not quite make it – was in the case of a young man charged with attempting to rape a nurse in her bedroom in the Western General's Nurses' Home. She said that she had wakened to find that a man had entered her bed and was disturbing her nightdress. She screamed, and he hurried out of her bedroom. The man pleaded not guilty, went to trial, and gave evidence. He admitted he had been in the nurse's bedroom but explained that he had entered the nurses' home simply with a view to stealing something, had found a bedroom door open, and had gone in. As he was looking for something to steal, the girl had awakened, so in order to stifle her screams and reassure her that he was only a thief, he had got into her bed, but had not in any other way disturbed her. In other words, other than theftuous, his intentions were wholly innocent.

Rather than stay and continue his reassurances, however, he fled from her room, rushed down the corridor and turned the corner through a door which he had thought would lead to the way out. But he had made a bad mistake. The door had opened into the sisters' common room! They decided that his intentions were less than innocent, and so did the jury. I sent him to prison for what was then the maximum period of two years.

But hope springs eternal in the heart of the offender seeking to persuade the court to accept what he says as being true. A 78-year-old man kept a very close check on what money he had. Daily he counted it, and recorded every item of income and expenditure. One day, two men who had once done a repair job for him returned to his house. They said his windows required to be painted and offered to do the job for £90. He said he might be prepared to pay them this, but the men were not too sure that he had as much cash as £90 handy. Proud of his solvency, the old man produced no less than £275 in notes 'to show them', as he put it. The two men went through the motions of doing the work and departed in their car, but were shortly after flagged down by police on the lookout for bogus workmen operating in the area. What should the police find but £275 in notes behind the door panel of their car?

Both men were charged with theft, but only one of them gave evidence. He said that they had told the old man that they were hoping to buy a van but couldn't afford it, and that he had then lent them £275 – without security or acknowledgment – to help them to buy it. But why, asked the procurator fiscal in cross-examination, had they put the money behind the door panel of their car? 'Well,' said the accused, with a perfectly straight face, 'there are a lot of thieves about these days!'

A similar situation arose in a trial of a young man for possessing cannabis. Police gave evidence that after a tip-off they had raided a house and arrested the accused. When he was searched, he was found to have a piece of cannabis in one of the pockets of his jacket, and a piece of joss stick in the other. Now drinkers will take peppermint to mask the smell of alcohol; and there was interesting evidence from the police that in the same way, joss sticks are sometimes burned because the smoke they produce counteracts the smell of cannabis smoke. The young man went to trial and gave evidence. How then, to explain the presence of the joss stick and the cannabis?

Well, he said that after he had finished at Art College he had been unable to get a job and had gone to a Buddhist monastery in Surrey for eighteen months. There, during periods of meditation, joss sticks were burned, partly to assist the process of meditation and partly to mark the passage of time. In the same way as the twenty-minute sucking time of a pan drop marked the passage of a Presbyterian sermon, so apparently did the hour's burning of a joss stick mark the passage of the meditation period. So that was why he had had the piece of joss stick in his pocket – a leftover from his meditating days in Surrey.

But what about the cannabis? 'Oh, that was easy,' he said. 'I'd just bought this jacket at a jumble sale the previous day, and the previous owner obviously hadn't bothered to turn his pockets out.' I might have believed his explanation about the joss stick or I might have believed his explanation about the cannabis. But to expect me to believe both was going rather too far. The *credo quia impossibile* test is a very high one, and this did not quite meet it either.

The clerks go on strike

In February 1979 the sheriff clerks and the court officers went on strike. This was unprecedented and almost as unthinkable as that the Sheriffs themselves should go on strike, but when the Sheriffs arrived for work they found a picket line across the door, no officers to take them into court and no clerks in the courts. The pickets did not seek to stop the Sheriffs from entering, and many of them looked distinctly embarrassed at finding themselves on the line, but they were not playing at strikes, they were and were solidly on strike. To call this 'industrial action' was even more inappropriate than in any ordinary strike. Clerks of court were industrious, certainly, but no one would ever have thought of them as being part of an industry; and total inaction scarcely qualifies as action. But the inaction was total, and a real crisis had arrived. What could the Sheriffs do without clerks and court officers? The answer was precious little. All that we could do was to deal with persons who had been arrested by the police and kept in custody overnight. The police brought them into court, and the Sheriff taking the court acted as his own clerk.

In the first few weeks of the strike, however, the Sheriffs met every day to review the situation and consider what other essential or near-essential work might be carried out without appearing to break the clerical strike. We met in Sheriff Martin Mitchell's room, and the atmosphere sometimes made me think of what it must have been like in the Führerbunker during the last days of the Third Reich. Here, as there, were out-of-work generals with only phantom armies to command, planning hopeless campaigns that could never get off the ground. And it was here, I think, that Sheriff Martin Mitchell emerged as the Martin we all got to know and love. He became aide-de-camp to the Sheriff Principal, liaison officer with the striking clerks, public relations officer to the outside world, organizer of the

Sheriffs' DIY clerking, mess secretary and teaboy generally. He became, in fact, the Bunkersmarshal – and a very good job he made of it too.

The strike, of course, was not just in Edinburgh. All over Scotland the wheels of justice ground to a halt. Emergency legislation was enacted to deal to some extent with the situation, but the Government did not appear to be in any hurry to deal with the *casus belli*, which, as in most strikes, was pay and conditions of employment. The Government appeared, in fact, to be quite content to let the strike drag on – and it did, for week after week. It was difficult to believe that this would have happened if the strike had been in England. Would the Government have been prepared to see the Old Bailey shut down indefinitely?

Through doing our own clerking we learned quite a lot! Perhaps we had never studied the wording of minute sheets or probation orders in any detail, but having to fill them in ourselves we discovered aspects of procedure which we had not fully appreciated before. As the strike went on we gradually did more and more than just deal with persons in custody, but through meetings with Sheriff Mitchell the clerks kept a watchful eye on what we did, it being tacitly understood that we worked only under their sufferance. Nowhere was a more watchful eye kept than in Glasgow. I learned that the striking clerks appointed one or two of their number to sit in the public benches of the one or two courts that they allowed to operate there to see that the Sheriffs were not extending the scope of their work beyond what the clerks considered to be permissible limits. Thus was turned upside down the great maxim underlying all the work of the courts – justice must not only be done, but must be manifestly seen to be done. The maxim in Glasgow had become 'justice must not only not be done, but must be manifestly seen not to be done'!

When it all came to an end after some three months, with slight improvements in the clerks' pay and conditions, two things were apparent. Firstly, there was no unpleasantness. No animosity was shown by the clerks to the Sheriffs, no rancour was shown by the Sheriffs to the clerks. Good-humoured normal relations were resumed very quickly. But secondly, there was an enormous backlog of cases waiting to be heard. So much so, that many summary cases were just quietly forgotten about, and the fiscals got into the habit of accepting absurdly reduced pleas of guilty in summary and solemn cases simply to get rid of as many of them as they decently could.

The law loves precedents. So I will only say that when the clerks again went on strike in 1981 we simply looked up our files on strike procedure and proceeded accordingly.

Sheriffs' meetings

Meetings of the Edinburgh Sheriffs took place from time to time. Originally they were held in Martin Mitchell's room, but they tended to get rather out of hand, partly because everybody talked at the same time and partly because of the difficulty of sitting comfortably in Martin's room, which became famous for the Himalayan ranges of paper, books, files, gadgets and bric-a-brac which littered all available surfaces. So the meetings moved to the Conference Room and took place in relatively formal fashion, with agendas and minutes. Most of the topics discussed, however, were domestic – it was seldom that matters of law were raised. Curiously, although Sheriffs enjoyed informally talking shop at a small gathering as much as any other shopkeepers, it was all very anecdotal. The Conference Room did not, for example, hear discussion of what sentencing policy might be followed in particular circumstances, but did hear what sentences particular Sheriffs had imposed in these circumstances in the past. And it was very seldom that we privately sought advice from each other on what to do in particular cases – no doubt we had all been thoroughly grounded in the doctrine that we were independent judges required to make up our own minds and responsible for applying our own discretion as we thought fit within the law.

Cameras in court

So many clerks, so many fiscals – by the time you had got to know who they were they had often enough moved on elsewhere. I tried to write down descriptions of them in my court diary so as to help me remember their names. I tried also to write down descriptions or make sketches of witnesses who had given evidence in civil cases where their evidence had been taken down in shorthand, so as to make the witnesses' typescript evidence come alive when I saw it some four or five weeks later. Alas, I had no talent for sketching, my efforts always producing the same unisex identikit blur of a face.

How much easier it would have been if witnesses had been officially photographed after they had taken the oath! But there was always a reluctance to allow cameras in the courtroom. Obviously, to preserve the dignity of the court, there could never be a free-for-all with cameras clicking at random, but I always thought it absurd that newspapers should have to publish only 'artist's impressions' of a court scene, when an official court photographer could have provided an accurate representation. Perhaps this will come about in due course, for in 1993 Lord President Hope, for a series of television documentaries, allowed cameras to enter the courtrooms to film criminal trials in progress. When the documentaries were shown nationwide it was months after the cases had been heard, and I would certainly not advocate the transmission of trials as they happen, such would be the unfair stress to which those taking part would be exposed.

For these documentaries, however, everyone had to consent to being filmed – accused, lawyers, judge and jury. If one juror was unwilling to be seen on screen, then none of the jury was shown. The cameras were not particularly intrusive, but they did provide a small problem. Normally two temptations afflict those on the Bench: the temptation to preach, and the temptation to make jokes, the latter being sometimes quite a pressing temptation, for the Sheriff has a captive audience. But once you were aware that the cameras were pointing at you and whirring over, along came another temptation – the temptation to try to look intelligent and to present an aura of gravitas, in other words playing to the cameras.

A series of six programmes was eventually shown. They were criticised for making court proceedings into an entertainment, but I did not think this criticism was valid. The whole purpose behind making the programmes was educational, so that people could see what actually happened in actual cases in actual courts. Of necessity only edited extracts of trials could be shown (jury trials could last many days); but if the programmes were entertaining, this would not necessarily detract from their educational value.

The newer practitioners

One of the very noticeable changes on returning to Edinburgh from Hamilton was the number of solicitors' firms which had amalgamated, had shortened their names, or had left the scene altogether. Another, which I did not welcome, was the rise of firms which proclaimed themselves to be simply 'defence lawyers'. On the other hand, there was a change for the better on the part of most of the up-market firms, who previously had considered Sheriff Court work to be beneath their dignity, farming out any such cases that came their way to down-market firms; now all of them had their own Sheriff Court specialists. Most of the young solicitors who appeared in the Sheriff Court – and not many above the age of forty were regular practitioners – were knowledgeable and able. The general level of performance was higher than it had been during my time at the Bar, but so it should have been, with law students spending their University days uninterrupted by concurrent office work as an apprentice, and having also to study for a diploma in practice. More and more lady lawyers began to appear, reflecting the fact that there had come to be more women than men studying law at University. The ladies concentrated on civil work in court, and, indeed, about the only redeeming feature of the otherwise arid experience of taking the summary civil court, when some twenty to thirty solicitors would be in attendance, was just to see, as one Sheriff put it, 'what new girls had turned up today'.

The older practitioners

The best of the lady lawyers who appeared before me, however, did so in the criminal court. She was one of the procurators fiscal, Mrs Margaret Kernohan. Tall and handsome, she had a commanding presence. She was scrupulously fair, and presented her cases with a clarity of expression which was a pleasure to listen to. Kind to nervous witnesses and inexperienced solicitors, she also easily held her own in dealing with the old guard of defending solicitors when they engaged in their ploys of forensic gamesmanship. Among that old guard I received particularly good value from appearances by Gordon McBain, whose cases were meticulously prepared and presented with a Columbo-like persistence, by George More, solemn and ever alert to detect police irregularities, by Vincent Belmonte, genial and broad-minded, and by Ray Megson, who had a twinkle in one eye and a glint of steel in the other, as befitted a man who in his time had refereed rugby internationals between England and Wales. There were, of course, some solicitors who did not make my heart sing when I saw them coming into court, but one who always brought good cheer with him was Patrick Wheatley, whose eye-contact was hard to resist when he was making a plea-in-mitigation.

Pleas-in-mitigation tended to have much in common. I seemed to have heard the same things said over and over again. Eventually I wrote a song which could be used as a plea-in-mitigation for all circumstances:–

> *May it please your Lordship, my plea will be quite brief,*
> *But loaded with emotion, full of glory and of grief.*
> *Please look upon my client in a sympathetic light,*
> *More sinned against than sinning was my hapless client's plight.*

> *For he hardly heard the whisper of temptation's wily voice,*
> *The fates conspired against him, no, he hadn't any choice.*
> *He didn't mean to do it, he'd no criminal intent,*
> *He panicked, he was stupid, it was just an ac-ci-dent!*

> *He has an aged mother and a statutory wife,*
> *And another wife at common law who complicates his life.*
> *They all are quite dependent on him, he's their sole support,*
> *Oh, do not take him from them now, oh may it please the Court!*

> *And then, he's got six children and another on the way,*
> *They need a father-figure, for their father rules, OK?*
> *Without him they'd be helpless, and a burden on the State,*
> *Whatever else you do to him, please don't incarcerate!*

> *He's got a lot on HP, and has huge arrears of rent,*
> *His moveables were poinded, they've all been and gone and*
> *went.*
> *The job he starts on Monday will have two weeks' lying-time,*
> *Whatever else befalls him, he just cannot pay a fine!*

But he's promised now to exercise the greatest self-restraint,
Probation would be wasted, for he's near enough a saint.
And so I ask your Lordship that the case should be dismissed
By putting up my client for the New Year's Honours List!

Some of my colleagues

I had many agreeable colleagues during my twenty years in Edinburgh. *Prima inter pares*, of course, was Isabel Sinclair, with whom it was a great pleasure to be reunited after our days together in Airdrie. To begin with I shared a room with Kenneth Middleton, a quiet scholarly man; he and Lord Cameron were appointed before a retiring age was brought in, and so they were entitled to go on for ever. Lord Cameron stayed on the Bench until he was eighty-six, but Kenneth Middleton took early retirement at eighty-two – not that he felt that he was too old for the job, but simply because he was getting married. Ronnie Ireland was erudition personified, in the classics and in the law, and became a very impressive Sheriff Principal in the Highlands. Neil Macvicar and Bill Hook exchanged ironic laughter with both style and class; they were great fun to be with. Of Martin Mitchell I have already spoken. But I should add that so essential a part was he of Edinburgh Sheriff Court that even after his retirement he continued to act as the Sheriffs' mess secretary. Gordon Shiach's gentle manner belied a firmness of purpose and an extraordinary capacity for work – in many legal and quasi-legal bodies apart from his normal work on the Bench. Isabel Anne Poole and John Horsburgh were such nice people that it was hard to believe that they were the most severe of us as sentencers. Andrew Bell was larger than life, worth a guinea a minute. Hazel Aronson (later Lady Cosgrove) radiated charm, and Roger Craik's dynamic grin complemented Dick Scott's engaging smile. These were some of the regulars in my time, and their company was a major fringe benefit of the job.

Presiding over us as Sheriff Principal were, in turn, Bill Bryden, Freddie O'Brien and Gordon Nicholson. Bill had a most dignified presence but was always approachable and affable. Freddie was such a good-humoured person that it was almost a pleasure to be overturned by him; he did it so nicely – 'I regret that I have to differ from the learned Sheriff.' Gordon was the most serious-minded. All three were excellent lawyers and highly respected by the whole Sheriff Court Bench and Bar.

Just as we were all sociable at the Bar, so were we all sociable on the Sheriff Court Bench. The Edinburgh Sheriffs held an annual party, and the occasion when it was held at my house was particularly memorable. My wife is a piano teacher, and for performance at the party she trained four of us to play an arrangement of Weber's *Invitation to the Waltz* for eight hands on two pianos. The four pianists were Freddie O'Brien, whose wife is Canadian, Neil Macvicar, whose wife is Greek, Gordon Nicholson, whose wife is English, and myself, whose wife is Icelandic. (The Sheriffdom has seen several other wives from other lands, oddly enough. Sheriff Principal Sinclair Shaw's wife was French, so is the wife of Marcus Stone, Willie McIlwraith's was Norwegian, George Presslie's is Swedish.) This cosmopolitan state of affairs has led me to reply to the question 'How do you get to be a Sheriff in Edinburgh?' 'Well, it helps if you can (a) play the piano and (b) have a wife who is not Scottish!'

Identification

Identification of accused persons in court presents no problems for the police. They know the accused will be in the dock and are 100 per cent certain of their identification. Not so, however, with civilian witnesses.

Two youths were charged with assaulting and insulting a Punjabi shopkeeper. The victim gave evidence through a Punjabi interpreter. In due course he was asked if he could identify his assailants – 'Look around the court and see if you can recognize the men who assaulted you.' This was translated into Punjabi, and his reply translated back into English. A smile broke over the interpreter's face as she gave his answer: 'I'm sorry, I can't. All white men look alike to me.' Collapse of Crown case!

I must have heard several thousand police officers give evidence. I am glad to say that I found at least 85 per cent of them to be good men and true, reliable, honest and often the 'salt-of-the-earth'. This of course implies that some 15 per cent were less than good in some way. Sometimes they were evasive, sometimes they appeared to have acted in a high-handed manner, sometimes they had just seemed unintelligent, and sometimes they were simply incredible.

When I found police officers incredible, it was often enough in their evidence of identification. 'Do you see the man in question here today?' the fiscal would ask. 'Point to him if you do.' Invariably and without hesitation, police officers would point to the man in the dock. 'That's him, sir.' But of course all police officers know that the man in question is sitting in the dock, and although there was generally no problem in accepting such identification evidence when the officers had been involved to any significant extent with the man in question, often enough they had had only a brief encounter with him, many months previously. How, I often wondered, how could they possibly have remembered him after such a long time?

I myself was occasionally interviewed by detectives when the fiscal was contemplating a prosecution for perjury arising from a summary trial where I had presided, the interview being with a view to my giving evidence of what the alleged perjurer had actually said at the trial where he had given evidence before me. I would consult my notebook and tell the detective what I had noted the man as having said. The detective would then thank me and add a throwaway line – 'and I take it you would have no difficulty in identifying him?' To which I always had to reply, 'I'm sorry, I have no recollection of what he looks like.' This was for the simple reason that although it was only two or three weeks previously that this person had been in the witness box, and the object of my close attention for ten or more minutes, I had seen scores of other persons in court since then and, unless they had had some great peculiarity of appearance or speech, I had had no particular reason for remembering any of them.

The very last summary trial I took threw up this problem yet again, and was a case where identification was crucial. Two police officers had stopped a motorist and had spoken to him for five minutes. They had never seen him before and had not seen him again since. Yet at his trial eighteen months later, they were asked to identify him and did so without hesitation. This was to be expected, for never once in thirty years of trials did I ever have a police officer fail to identify the accused. But a brief encounter, five minutes long and eighteen months ago – how many thousands of other persons would they have encountered in that time? That one of them should have been able to remember the accused's unremarkable features over that length of time would have been astonishing: that two of them should have been able to remember him was quite incredible. I had no hesitation in returning a verdict of not guilty.

Dry humour

When the new courthouse was nearing completion and people asked if I were not contemplating retirement, my standard reply was that I could not retire until I had had a shower – this meant, simply, that I wanted to spend some time in the new courthouse, where each of the Sheriffs' chambers was to have its own en suite facilities, including a shower. But it was difficult to think when it would be appropriate to take a shower – it was not as if one stayed on after work before changing for an evening engagement. So for my last day at Edinburgh Sheriff Court, not having yet taken advantage of this unexpected facility, I brought a bath towel to court and was all set to have a shower before I retired. I turned on the tap. Nothing happened! If it ever had worked, it too, like me, had now retired.

6

The Scottish Arts Council

A voluntary body

I was appointed a member of the Scottish Arts Council in 1978. There had always been a problem for members of such voluntary bodies in getting time off work to attend meetings, but since such appointments were made by the Secretary of State and since appointments of Sheriffs were also made by the Secretary of State, it followed that he must be willing to excuse my attendance at court any time my attendance was required at an Arts Council meeting.

The press and the public loved to hate the Arts Council. They perceived it to be not democratically elected, to be unrepresentative, and to spend its time wasting public money on fatuous nonsense. It was quite true that its members were not democratically elected to represent any particular constituency of artists or laymen. Most of its members were people whom the full-time Arts Council officers had come across in the course of their work – which work of course included their going round the country and feeling the pulse of artistic involvement. All along they kept an eye out to see which persons, both professional artists and interested laymen, would be likely to have some contribution to make to the administration and development of the arts in Scotland. If the Secretary of State accepted their recommendations and if those recommended were willing to accept his offer of unpaid work, then there they were for at least three years, entrusted with the spending of a large amount of taxpayers' money on things artistic.

Money was the driving force of the Council's life. It was seldom, in fact, that the Council talked about the arts *per se*; it was almost always about competing claims to the limited amount of available money. In my time the Council's work was done in departments dedicated to the different art forms – drama, music (which included dance), literature, art – and a department concerned with mixed art forms. Each department had a committee of Council members, and each had a full-time director. The committees made recommendations to the Council, and the Council made the decisions. But it was the department directors, in their recommendations to their committees, who effectively made all the real decisions on where the money should be spent.

Popular and unpopular music

My whole time was spent on the Music Committee. I was its chairman for five years, and this gave me a good deal of satisfaction, as I had never regarded myself as a musician proper. By that I mean that I was not a pure and professional classically trained and oriented musician as my wife Lolo is. My eldest brother Kenneth ran a dance band in his last years at school, and he brought me up on the popular songs of the 1930s and 40s. Indeed, if I had had to appear on my brother-in-law's *Mastermind* programme, I would have chosen these songs as my specialist subject. (I might mention in passing that I would not have scored anything like as well as Magnus's wife Mamie, who knows every word of every song.) Like so many other children I was given piano lessons from the age of seven, and like so many other children I wanted to give it all up at the age of twelve. But I then found that I could play by ear, and after that I never again had any thought of giving up the piano. For in these days anyone who could play the popular songs of the day on a piano was much in demand at parties and dances. But playing by ear did not mean giving up playing at sight, though altogether I probably spent only about one-quarter of my piano-playing time working at classical pieces. One-quarter would be spent on my own compositions, and about one-half playing, or working out arrangements of, great popular songs such as 'That old black magic', 'April in Paris' or 'Night and day'. I also found that I enjoyed singing, and all my life I have taken great pleasure in singing everything from hymns to jazz songs, from love songs to unrequited love songs, in family gatherings and in choirs, in glee clubs and in choral societies.

But the Music Committee of the Arts Council was not concerned with popular music. It might be said that its concern was with *unpopular* music. The theory was that popular music will pay its own way. The public will flock to hear the rock and pop stars of the day, and will be unconcerned at the high prices they have to pay. Their music will continue without any need for government subsidy. But opera and ballet are extraordinarily expensive to put on, and the limited number of members of the public who want to hear and see opera and ballet could not reasonably afford the extraordinarily high prices they would have to pay if their seats were not subsidized by public money. Without audiences, the performing companies would wither and the art forms would eventually perish. So if, as an article of faith, it is considered that such art forms should not only be preserved but developed as among the finer achievements of the human condition, unpopular in the wider context though they might be, public money would have to be found for them.

It would also have to be found for new compositions. Modern music – that is, music which is modern relative to whatever has become established – has always had a hard struggle to survive until it does become established. It is thought of as spiky, barbarous, unplayable or offensive to the civilized ear. Thus, to begin with, Beethoven, thus, more than a century later, Stravinsky. It is very much a minority taste. So too is chamber music, which has been cynically described as 'music written for very small audiences'. If such music is to continue to be written and played, it is likely to require subsidy from public funds, for composers have to live, and until they acquire national standing as composers they cannot depend on box-office returns for their livelihood.

So a reasonable amount of money went into the support of new music, whether it was the performing group or the composer that was new. Established composers were also supported when new works were commissioned from them by performing groups or other bodies. The commissioners would meet part of the composer's fee and the Arts Council would meet the rest. I was surprised to discover one of the ways in which an appropriate fee for composers was quantified. In many cases they were paid not for the length of time spent composing their new piece, but for the length of the piece itself – so much per minute of playing time!

Festivals were supported, as were activities as diverse as piping, non-commercial jazz, Gaelic song, electronic music and concerts by the Council for Music in Hospitals. By far the largest amount of Arts Council money spent on music, however, was that spent on the national companies, which in my time were Scottish Opera, the Scottish National Orchestra, Scottish Ballet, the Scottish Chamber Orchestra and the Scottish Baroque Ensemble. They were perpetually in a state of financial crisis. The reason was simple. It was not a case of them living beyond their means, it was a case of them not really having the means to live properly at all. Now the Scottish Arts Council got its money from what was then the Arts Council of Great Britain, which in turn got its money from the United Kingdom Department of Education. One hundred years ago, the 'Goschen formula' was devised to regulate the distribution of United Kingdom money between England and Scotland, giving roughly seven-eighths to England and one-eighth to Scotland. This worked reasonably well across the whole board in the sphere of music – except in the case of the national companies. The difficulty, as it seemed to me, was that Scotland was too large a country not to have national companies, but was too small a country to maintain them on what was available for music under the Goschen formula.

The national companies

This became one of my hobby-horses. I liked to refer to the national companies as the new 'Honours of Scotland'. But the Arts Council of Great Britain appeared to think only of England-based companies as being national companies. The English national companies did reasonably well with the money available for music under the Goschen formula. But if the 7:1 ratio properly applied to national companies as well as everything else, then England should have had seven orchestras of the size and standing of the Scottish National Orchestra, seven Scottish Chamber Orchestras, seven Scottish Operas and seven Scottish Ballets. Certainly England did have seven orchestras comparable to the SNO and the SCO, but it did not have seven Scottish Operas or seven Scottish Ballets. But Scotland had one of each, and could never get enough money to keep them going properly.

Scottish Opera, hugely expensive at the best of times, was our principal headache, a headache eased not one whit by its Artistic Director, the celebrated Peter Ebert. He wanted the best. If a harpsichord had to be used on stage as part of the props, he would want it to be inlaid with real gold leaf and not just painted to look as if it were gold-leafed. Never mind the expense! The world's best should be engaged as soloists. Never mind their fees! But I did mind their fees, which I thought were absurd. Of course the leaders in a profession should expect to receive more than the journeymen. I would have no quarrel at all with the Dean of the Faculty of Advocates receiving twice the going rate for senior counsel for a run-of-the-mill reparation proof or the President of the Royal College of Surgeons receiving twice the fee for performing a common-or-garden appendectomy. But for an operatic diva to receive *ten* times what an ordinary soprano would get for a run-of-the-mill common-or-garden *Bohème* grieved me greatly, and I made it another of my hobby-horses to campaign wherever I could against the wholly ridiculous level of fees which the star prima donnas both sought and got. If nothing else, it must have made the members of the chorus feel very inadequate; and since only a minority in any audience would notice any difference in quality between the performance of a star and the performance of a top-class singer not rated as a star, it showed that people did not really go to hear opera but went to see stars. But the star system appeared to be endemic in Europe. If one house sought to reduce overall costs by reducing the stars' fees to reasonable levels, other houses would look askance at such stars as accepted reasonable fees and cease to engage them.

Although money was the dominant topic at committee meetings, there was much cheerful reporting of performances and performers, for we were all encouraged to attend concerts as much as we could, at the Council's expense. All the members of the committee apart from myself were professional musicians or concert promoters, and when necessary I sought to justify my position as chairman by saying that I was a neutral lawyer who tried to keep the peace among the musicians. But they were a peaceful company, and there was usually no difficulty in accepting the recommendations of the music department's director, Christie Duncan. He was a walking encyclopedia of the Scottish music scene, attended endless concerts and observed endless board meetings of the national companies. He was also, in general terms, a highly civilized and witty man. We met usually once a week and had a lot of laughs together. Sometimes people asked me what it meant to say that he was the director and I was the chairman – what exactly was our relationship? I had no difficulty in referring them to the *Yes, Minister* television programme – I was the weak, vain, vacillating, amateur politician, Jim Hacker, while Christie was the all-wise, shrewd and cunning professional civil servant, Sir Humphrey.

Arts guilds and music clubs

It was presumably my experience with Strathaven Arts Guild which had brought me on to the Council in the first place, and so I not unnaturally took a particular interest in the other arts guilds and music clubs up and down the land. It was the Music Committee which recommended what size of grants they should be given, and in considering their applications for assistance, I found myself as poacher turned gamekeeper.

These bodies were and are a splendid feature of cultural life in Scotland, providing the opportunity for local people to hear and see top-class artists in local settings, typically in village halls, and at affordable seat prices as a result of subsidies by the Arts Council and the local authority. It was a popular misconception that the Arts Council decided which artists should perform at the various clubs. On the contrary, each club devised its own programme, normally five or six events a year, and paid the artists themselves from their box-office takings, topped up (often heavily) from their Arts Council grant and from their local authority grant. Clubs soon got to know what type of events and concert programmes would be acceptable to the Music Committee for grant purposes. It was partly a question of which artists from the non-commercial sector were chosen and partly the size of their fees. A programme consisting of five concerts of Country and Western music would not be acceptable, nor would a programme including one concert by an operatic prima donna. The former would be considered commercially viable without any subsidy, the latter would be unrealistically expensive.

Scottish Opera's orchestras

There were many meetings with the boards of the national companies, trying to resolve their differences and simply to keep them afloat. A recurring problem was that of orchestral accompaniment for Scottish Opera. When it was founded, the intention had been that the Opera would perform when the SNO would otherwise have been resting, and that the SNO would play for the Opera, and thus in effect become the Opera orchestra. But this arrangement did not last for long. The SNO found it too constricting to its ambitions, and in due course a new orchestra altogether, the Scottish Chamber Orchestra, was founded. Its purpose was primarily to act as the pit orchestra for the Opera, but it was intended that it would give concerts in its own right when the Opera was resting – the reverse of the SNO situation. Further, the SCO would be more flexible, for it would be an orchestra where the players were not salaried under a contract, but were fee-earning, hired for each performance. Thus in theory the SCO could have different players each time it appeared: in practice they were usually the same players most of the time.

The relationship between the SCO and the Opera did not fare much better than the previous relationship between the SNO and the Opera. Peter Ebert, the Opera's chief executive, was an *éminence grise*; the SCO's chief executive was the then *enfant terrible* Michael Storrs. Each was ambitious for his company, and found it difficult to reconcile proposed performance dates. The SCO became impatient with being hidden in the pit, and wanted to perform more and more as a concert-giving orchestra in its own right. The Opera became impatient with the SCO, and wanted to have its own contracted in-house orchestra. Eventually the matter was resolved by what might be called an unexpected *coup de théâtre*. Without prior notification to the Arts Council, Scottish Opera simply went ahead and – more or less overnight – formed its own orchestra. This led to a further round of strained relations. Relations between the Opera and the SCO immediately improved – neither was any longer dependent on the other – but relations between the Opera and the Arts Council deteriorated. Where was the money to come from to meet the cost of this new orchestra? Somehow or other, after much heart-searching and head-scratching, the cost was accommodated into the budget, but in due course the Opera orchestra itself became dissatisfied with being always hidden in the pit, and sought to set up its own programme as a concert-giving orchestra. The result was that Scotland had just too many professional orchestras, for of course the BBC Scottish Symphony Orchestra was also in the field as a concert-giving orchestra.

When I say 'too many professional orchestras' I mean too many to be properly supported on the public money available for their support and on the available market. And I use the phrase 'available market' with distaste. I never liked the fact that money was such a major factor in the music world. I would have preferred it if performers could have performed for the sheer pleasure of it, and if 'good states of mind' could have been the watchword instead of 'bums on seats'.

There was never anything like the amount of money which we would have liked to have had at our disposal to do all the things for music in Scotland which we would have liked to have done. It had all been very different, and exciting, in the 1960s when there had been money 'to play with', and new things could be developed. But it had all become defensive. Instead of starting new things we simply had to try to keep the old things going.

Amateur musicians

If money had been no object, however, I would have liked to have seen a good deal of it expended on development of amateur music-making. Amateur music-making is by definition a love affair. Amateurs play or sing not to make a living but to express and enhance their living. Nor do all amateurs need an audience. Their primary concern is to obtain those good states of mind which an intellectually and viscerally satisfying love affair can bring. If this is so, does the amateur need the Arts Council? Do quangos know about love affairs? Can the arrival of good amateur states of mind be bureaucratically assisted? Or can the amateurs just be left to find their own level and get on with it in their own time? Over the years the amateur as consumer, has, of course, been very well served by the Council, which has been responsible for so much professional music being made, and being made accessible to him, not just for his enjoyment but to set standards for him to aspire to. But as performer, the Council has largely left him to his own devices, apart from putting money into amateur opera companies and the National Federation of Music Societies.

Obviously the encouragement of amateurs must start in school. But how often the involvement and enthusiasm of the early teens is lost with the arrival of the later teens! What is there to take over when the structure of school music is left behind? Well, the Council might like to consider how the chain of music clubs and arts guilds which it supports up and down the land might be used to assist amateur music. Who are better placed to promote amateur musical activity? There must be many frustrated singers because the only choirs in their community are church choirs, and if they do not belong to these churches they will not be able to sing in concert with others. Again, there may be frustrated would-be chamber players, frustrated simply because they have not met and do not know how to meet others in the same condition. Could their local club or guild not set up a performers' section?

But there are not nearly enough music clubs and arts guilds in Scotland. What I would like to see, accordingly, is the Arts Council appointing an officer charged with the responsibility of promoting amateur music, and then extending what was John Knox's revolutionary sixteenth-century educational concept of a school in every parish into that of an arts centre in every parish, providing facilities as much for local amateurs to enjoy 'doing their own thing' as to enjoy listening to the visiting professionals. Sir Arthur Quiller-Couch reminded us that

> *Brave lads, in olden musical centuries*
> *Sang night by night adorable choruses;*
> *Sat late by ale-house doors in April,*
> *Chaunting with joy as the moon was rising.*

That strikes me as summing up the fun of amateur music, be it choral or instrumental, and I would like to think that a new musical century will see its own brave lads singing and playing, together or by themselves, as the most normal and natural thing in the world.

Two recurring problems

If the Music Committee had its trials and tribulations with various clients, so had the Council itself. The two which occupied a particularly extensive amount of thinking time were Ricky de Marco and Ian Hamilton Finlay, both exceptionally talented men. Most Council members recognised Ricky's extraordinary creative and imaginative energy, his zeal as an evangelist for the arts, his gifts as a draughtsman and his dogged determination to keep his gallery going in the face of repeated setbacks. He was helped enormously by a sunny disposition and an engaging smile. But he was deeply hindered by a difficulty in appreciating that budgets are designed to control expenditure. As with music in general, so with Ricky in particular – I often wished that money did not have to come into the arts at all! It seemed all wrong that, like Orson Welles, Ricky had to waste so much of his time and energy in raising money when he could have been devoting it to creating new artistic projects. And it never seemed quite right for the Arts Council to have to keep on delivering homilies to him on the necessity of making his gallery's ends meet – though of course it was the Council's duty to do so.

The other main headache was brought on by Ian Hamilton Finlay. He is a highly gifted artist, sculptor and poet, with an international reputation. But he hated the Arts Council and all its works. It was not a question of the Council not giving him financial support for his work, but, among other things, of not giving him moral support in his running battle with Strathclyde Regional Council over payment of local rates. He had created a widely acclaimed sculpture garden called Little Sparta on what was otherwise a bleak hillside at Dunsyre in Lanarkshire; and he described the house where he lived and to which the garden was attached as a 'garden temple'. The Regional Council said it was rateable, as a commercial art gallery. He said it was exempt from rates as an artistic temple and refused to pay. The law provided, however, that to be exempt from rates the temple would have to be occupied by a religious body or an arts body and not by an individual. Proceedings were duly taken in Lanark Sheriff Court by the Regional Council, and decree for payment was inevitably granted against him. When sheriff officers duly arrived at the garden temple to enforce the decree they were met by a defiant

Finlay and a delighted congregation from the press; and what became known as the Battle of Little Sparta began. Various sculptures were eventually poinded, i.e. impounded or marked down by sheriff officers with a view to sale for the benefit of the Regional Council, but they could only be sold if it was clear that they belonged to Finlay. Finlay maintained, however, that he had sold or otherwise disposed of them to third parties, and disputes about their ownership rumbled on for year after year; as far as I know they have never been satisfactorily resolved.

Whether the rates were ever paid I do not know, but I do remember the way in which the Arts Council's principal officers were harassed by Finlay in letters and late-night phone-calls. I would certainly not have wished to have entered into correspondence with him since he used language in a different way from other people and his reasoning process was unique unto himself. 'Moderation in all things' was not a maxim he applied, and some of the things he did would have been seen as endearing schoolboy pranks had they not been essentially malevolent. Thus he had headed notepaper printed bearing the legend 'Every time I hear the words "Scottish Arts Council" I reach for my water pistol'; he sent all members of the Council tin badges bearing the letters 'SAC – KGB'; and he staged a demonstration outside the Council's headquarters in Edinburgh's Charlotte Square with a placard inscribed '*Mors concilio Artium*'. A brilliant artist, no doubt, but to the Arts Council Finlay was also *a sair fecht*.

All very nice

Headaches apart, membership of the Arts Council was very pleasant, in that one met such a large number of able people, on the Council and in the field. As we were encouraged to see and hear as much as we reasonably could of what went on in the field of the arts, we had the opportunity of visiting all sorts of venues (horrid word), which for the Music Committee meant everything from opera houses to jazz cellars, via village halls and salons in stately homes. Meetings of the Council were all very *nice*, so much so that consensus was the order of the day, for it would not have been nice to have called for a vote. I recall only one vote, which I myself called for. This arose from an unhappy situation in or about 1982. After we had made our offers of grants to our clients and these had been accepted, the Government announced a cut in its grant to the Council. The Council's Director then proposed writing to all our clients, saying, 'As a result we regret that we have no option but to reduce the amount of our grant to you.' I felt that this was quite wrong. Once an offer has been accepted, a contract exists. I said that we did have an option, and that was to honour our contracts. In the interests of the morality of keeping our promises, the legality of keeping our contracts and above all keeping intact the credibility of the Council, we should decline to accept the Director's proposal. No matter that our own grant was to be cut – did we not have substantial reserves? What are reserves for but to be kept against a rainy day? And when the Government cut our grant was it not raining heavily? So I pressed for a vote, but, alas, was unsuccessful in persuading the majority to go along with me.

My favourite music

David Dorward, a leading Scottish composer, was a member of the Music Committee. He worked with the BBC and at one time ran a programme called *Autograms* where people would be asked to play and talk about their favourite records. It was a sort of *Desert Island Discs* without the interviews and the luxuries. He asked me to take part in it, and inevitably it was a very difficult task to choose seven favourite pieces to play. For the record, the pieces I eventually chose and was very happy to talk about were Chopin's Scherzo No. 2 in B flat minor, Rex Stewart and his Footwarmers' 'Finesse', Handel's Recorder Sonata in A minor, Duke Ellington's 'Take the A Train', The King's Singers singing about themselves, the Adagio from Mozart's Divertimento in B Flat major, and Chabrier's *España*.

If I could only have taken one of them, it would have been Chabrier's *España*, for that marvellous work encapsulates for me the eventual joyousness of music, even as the four lines of verse I quoted from Sir Arthur Quiller Couch captures for me the eventual joyousness of song. And this is what I think that all the work of the Arts Council should lead to – joy in the morning, and in the evening, joy.

7

Peebles Sheriff Court

A gentler court

In 1983 I became the senior Sheriff at Edinburgh, and as one of the perks of that position I was appointed to take the weekly court at Peebles on a Wednesday. So I went there in succession to Neil Macvicar, and the twelve years that I had there until my retirement were, I think, the happiest of my whole time in the law. The pace and tone of the Peebles court was so much more gentle and civilized than the hurly-burly of Edinburgh. In other words, Peebles had a better class of malefactors, and drugs were not a standard feature of its life. Taking the court in Peebles must be the Edinburgh Sheriff's equivalent of the experience enjoyed by an Anglican clergyman normally ministering to a tough East End parish in London but occasionally asked to take evensong in a quiet Sussex village. 'Peebles for pleasure' has long been a tourist trade slogan: certainly for me it was a case of Peebles for judicial pleasure.

The local practitioners were also gentle and civilized, the clerks became good friends, and I was particularly fortunate in that the procurator fiscal, Fergus Brown, had been a personal friend ever since we had been students together in the same year of the Edinburgh University Law Faculty. I have rarely known a man so well-beloved as Fergus. All solicitors invariably spoke warmly of him, and to walk down the High Street of Peebles with him was a revelation – every other citizen would greet him and he them.

The friendliness of the courthouse was rather nicely expressed by the situation surrounding one of the sheriff clerks. A dog-breeder on the side, he used to bring two of his beautiful

King Charles spaniels to spend the day with him in his office. His superiors in the civil service heard about this and indicated that he should not bring his dogs to work. I am not a dog-lover myself, but I knew the value of these dogs to the court, and I stoutly defended his having his dogs there. For the solicitors would come into the office, pat the dogs on the head and pass the time of day with them; the old lags would come into the office to pay their fines, pat the dogs on the head and pass the time of day with them. What the dogs did was help to cement the happy-family feeling of the court.

Peebles must be the prettiest town in the Borders, and its High Street is a delight. Three buildings stand together at its west end, being, by a curious quirk of town-planning, the courthouse, the Parish Church and a mock-Tudor Chinese restaurant, providing among them for body, mind and spirit. The courthouse was quite an impressive building on the outside, but inside – particularly in its main stairwell – it radiated all the gloom of a mid-Victorian funeral parlour. Dark varnish was everywhere. The courtroom contained what must have been one of the most uncomfortable docks in the land – a wooden plank to sit upon and another plank at 90 degrees for the back to rest against – and it came as a great relief to hear that the courtroom was to be modernized.

In the dock

It took several months for the work to be carried out, and during that time the court sat in the former Burgh Chambers. This was a very interesting experience, for there was no dock there at all. Now I had long felt that the lack of a dock was one of the few things we could usefully borrow from the criminal court system in America – accused persons there sit at a table beside their lawyer while the procurator fiscal's opposite number, the district attorney, sits with his assistant at an adjacent table. If nothing else, this makes identification much more realistic. Witnesses are not 'assisted' in their identification as they can be in a summary trial in Scotland by the fact that the accused sits alone in a special enclosure. Further, in a jury trial, the accused in Scotland will sit in this special enclosure with a uniformed policeman on either side, and I always used to think that it required a remarkable elasticity of mind on the part of a jury to presume that the accused person was innocent despite his being seen set apart and sitting between officers wearing their caps and sometimes carrying truncheons in their white-gloved hands.

During the refurbishment of the Peebles courtroom, we all were obliged to sit round one large oval table – Sheriff, sheriff clerk, fiscal, defence lawyer and accused, and we got on perfectly well. I tried to persuade the Administration not to have a dock in the new courtroom, but was unsuccessful. I was also unsuccessful in trying to persuade them to do away with the traditional semi-circular table in the well of the court, with the witness box and the fiscal at one side and the jury box and the defending solicitor at the other – this has meant that either the fiscal or the defending solicitor has his back to either the witness or the jury at all times. But I was successful in persuading them not to have a fixed jury box at all. There had been a spell of fourteen years when only two jury trials took place in Peebles, and the jury box took up so much space that for the normal Wednesday court solicitors had to climb over each other to get a seat at the table. So a row of seven chairs was provided, normally used by the press and the court social workers, and if a jury trial did take place – and I think there were three that I presided over – then a row of eight other chairs was placed in front of the seven and the whole enclosed with a removable balustrade.

The Beltane Festival

The parish church next door to the courthouse has a wide flight of steps leading up to it which makes a splendid setting for the crowning of 'the village queen' during the annual Beltane week's celebrations in June. The steps are large enough to accommodate all the town's primary school children, who enter with great gusto into the elaborate ceremony. They parade in fancy dress through the town and take up their positions on the steps to witness the arrival of the Beltane Queen and her coronation by a distinguished local lady, who one year was none other than the then Peebles Sheriff, Isabel Sinclair. The whole affair was a lovely sight to see, as all the children were in fancy dress, as mice, gollywogs, pirates, Red Indians, soldiers, sailors and so on according to their class in school.

All went well until the great gollywog crisis of 1991. A lady who had been a school teacher in Peebles but who had retired and now lived elsewhere wrote to the Beltane Committee to say that she felt that it was not appropriate to feature gollywogs in the procession, as this might be thought to have racial implications; and she enclosed a cheque for £50 to purchase other costumes for that particular school class to wear. This caused uproar. The town divided into two camps – 'We are non-racist, we are politically correct' on the one hand, and 'We want our gollywogs, we need our gollywogs' on the other. The local press ran the story gleefully for weeks and it reached the national press as well. Letters to the editor flowed thick and fast, the 'Move with the times' faction contending with the 'Aye beens'. The latter seemed to have the stronger voices, and indeed a local musician sold many cassettes containing his specially composed song 'I wanna be a golly in the Beltane parade'.

But the Beltane Committee reluctantly bowed to pressure from certain primary school teachers and settled for a soft-centred fudge in the form of costumes depicting ragdolls of a neutral hue. As the Beltane Festival approached, however, we held our breaths at the court, with strong rumours of impending actions of interdict on either side, and the likelihood of breaches of the peace when it was heard that a busload of men disguised as gollywogs had been sighted on a collision course to Peebles with a busload of National Front members. But the buses finally took their separate ways, no action by police or the court was required, and no interdicts were granted. A last stand of the traditionalists was made, however, at the fancy dance held on the night before the crowning ceremony, when about 100 Peebleans appeared happily attired as gollywogs. But not one appeared in the procession next morning. So it was goodbye gollywogs, and tears were shed, but at least no possible offence could have been caused to the black population of Peebles, for there was no such population.

Brown Brothers

One of the first civil cases I had in Peebles was an action of reparation where the owner of a large Fiat car was claiming damages from a farmer. The farmer was the owner of a cattle grid, one of the iron bars of which sprang up from its crumbling concrete seating when this Fiat was driven over it, knocking a hole in the car's engine sump. The engine oil poured out and the badly damaged car could go no further. I heard evidence from the car's owner and one or two others about what a very special limited-edition model this car had been; they all appeared to be suggesting that it was a rare collector's piece. One of the leading car dealers in Peebles is called Brown Brothers, and one of the brothers was a witness for the pursuer. He said he had sold the car to the pursuer, and gave evidence as to what repairing the vehicle would cost. Having heard so much about what a rare car this was, I asked Mr Brown, 'Where did you get it from? Who sold it to you?' I was distinctly taken aback when he looked fixedly at me and said, 'From you, my Lord.' I said, 'I'm sorry, I don't think you quite understood the question. The question was "From whom did you buy this car?"' To which he replied, 'Oh, from your Lordship.' I let that pass, but afterwards I met Mr Brown and pursued the matter further. It turned out that he had not met the previous owner but knew him to have been an Edinburgh lawyer called Nigel Thomson (a Writer to the Signet, now, alas, deceased); Mr Brown, having heard that I came from Edinburgh and knowing that Sheriffs were lawyers of a sort and that I was called Nigel Thomson, had put two and two together but had not got it quite right. I happened to need to change my own car at that time, and since Mr Brown appeared to be a very pleasant man and since he thought that he had bought a car from me, I thought that the least I could do was to buy a car from him. Which I did, and have been buying cars from Brown Brothers ever since.

Motoring offences

Sections 1, 2, 3, 5 and 6 of the Road Traffic Act 1972 created the standard motoring offences which frequently came before the Sheriff Court – causing death by reckless driving, reckless driving, careless driving, driving while impaired through drink or drugs, and driving with more than the permitted blood/alcohol level, which was 80 milligrammes of alcohol in 100 millilitres of blood. Off parade, I sometimes used to sing about it all:–

This old man's on Section One,
His car's as lethal as a gun.
With a nick-nock, in the dock,
Take him for a ride,
This old man is going inside.

This old man's on Section Two,
What a reckless thing to do!
With a nick-nock, in the dock,
Take him for a ride,
This old man's disqualified.

This old man's on Section Three,
He drove very careless-lee.
With a nick-nock, in the dock,
Didn't even stop!
This old man is totting – op!

This old man's on Section Five,
He's lucky just to be alive.
With a nick-nock, in the dock,
Have another drink?
Next time, chum, you're in the clink!

This old man's on Section Six,
Alcohol and blood don't mix.
With a nick-nock, in the dock,
Rotten luck, old chum,
This old man was only Eighty-one!

The Icelandic Judges

In 1986 some twenty members of the Icelandic Judges Association came on a week's study visit to Scotland. As my wife was the Consul for Iceland in Edinburgh, we took it upon ourselves to organize a programme for them. In Iceland stained-glass artistry is much prized, and so the judges' first day became a stained-glass Sunday. To St Giles in the morning, where over the main door at the cathedral's west end they saw the large window that celebrates Robert Burns. That there should be such a memorial window at all was remarkable, because at Burns's bicentenary in 1957, before he had been 'rehabilitated', the Burns Federation had asked the Cathedral Board if at least a commemorative plaque might be erected, and had had their request turned down on the curious grounds that there was insufficient space on the walls. But with the passage of time Burns had become acceptable, and to such an extent acceptable, that the main stained-glass window was replaced with one commemorating Burns's place in Scottish history. As remarkable was the choice of a leading Icelandic artist to design the window – one Leifur Breidfjord, who had studied at the Edinburgh College of Art. In the afternoon the judges were taken on a tour of the Trossachs, and on the way they visited Cornton Vale women's prison. There they saw the stained-glass window in the prison chapel, which happened to have been designed by the daughter of the President of the Icelandic Judges Association! The President was there in person to admire his daughter's handiwork with the rest of the party. His name was Asgeir Petursson, and his daughter's Systa Asgeirsdottir, which, incidentally, neatly illustrates the Icelandic system of naming children. A child does not take its father's surname as its own surname; its surname is its father's Christian name, adding 'son' or 'dottir' to it according to the child's gender.

It was surprising to find out quite how many members there were of the Icelandic Judges Association. Iceland then had a total population of just over a quarter of a million – roughly equal to that of Dundee, yet, although Dundee managed with just two Sheriffs at that time, there were no less than eighty members of the Icelandic Judges Association. This was roughly the same number as were then members of the Sheriffs' Association for the whole of Scotland, with its population of five million.

Why would this be the case? Such is the geography of Iceland that outside of Reykjavik about two-thirds of the population live in small isolated communities around the coasts, and the Icelandic equivalent of the Scottish Sheriff used to be much more like the Wild West Sheriff – being local police chief and local government chief executive as well as local judge. So apart from some half dozen High Court judges and an appropriate number of lower court judges in Reykjavik there had to be a large number of judges for the many little places around the circumference of the island. The other reason why there were so many Icelandic judges appeared to me to be because of all the writing they had to do in their summary criminal courts. When accused persons make their first appearance at courts of this type in Scotland they either plead not guilty, in which case a trial date is fixed, or plead guilty, in which case the Sheriff proceeds to sentence. Where the accused pleads guilty the fiscal says his piece, the defence solicitor says his piece, the Sheriff passes sentence and may say why he has passed the sentence in question. But whatever the plea, the only official writing throughout the whole process is done by the clerk of court, who minutes the date for trial or the sentence imposed. But in the Icelandic equivalent the judge has to write down all that the prosecutor says, then all that the defence lawyer says, and then has to write down his reasons for his decision on sentence. Given the great deal of time that this takes, it is no wonder that a large number of judges is required to get through all the work. When the Icelandic judges came to attend a sitting of the summary criminal court in Edinburgh and asked me how many cases I would have to deal with, I said there were probably about eighty cases on my list; they found this very hard to believe, saying that they would not be able to deal with more than about eight!

Since many of the Icelandic courts would be about the same size as the court in Peebles, it seemed wholly appropriate to take them there to see a small country court in action. They were entertained to lunch at his house by Bill Goodburn, the then Dean of the local Faculty, who had enjoyed a recent visit to Iceland, and then went off in their bus to visit what they were told, with tongue in cheek, was a typical country house of a typical Scottish Sheriff – the architectural extravaganza of Abbotsford, home of Sir Walter Scott, who, among other things, was Sheriff of Selkirk. The judges were very impressed to find that his library actually contained a number of books in Icelandic!

More than poaching

Fishing is important to Icelanders. Their national prosperity depends upon it. Fishing is also important to Peebleans. The river Tweed runs through the town, and the coat of arms of Peebles shows three salmon swimming. Not surprisingly, much time in the criminal court was spent on salmon poaching cases. But I only once heard poaching being pled as a defence.

Police at Peebles had received information that on 20th February 1992 there was likely to be a break-in to a big house that stood isolated on the banks of the Tweed some five miles from Peebles. And on 19th February they saw a Mr Peter Parkin, whom they knew as a Glasgow man with a criminal record, driving a car in Peebles. So on 20th February they set up an observation post outside the big house and waited to see what might happen. What had already happened was that the householder and his wife had gone to a dinner party in Edinburgh. What happened next was that about 6.45pm the same Allegro car as the one in which Mr Parkin had been seen the previous day drove past the house, came back and parked about 100 yards from the house. Two men got out. Some forty minutes later the police heard thumping noises and the sound of breaking glass. The police then entered through the broken back door, searched the house, and heard muffled voices on the top floor where the master bedroom was situated. The bedroom was in darkness. Switching on the light, they saw that two persons were hiding under the bed. One of them was Mr Parkin, the other a Mr Wilson. Both of them were wearing gloves and around them was furniture and drawers in disarray. They were at once arrested, and were carried out through the broken kitchen door to the police vehicles.

Both men pleaded not guilty and went to trial. Mr Wilson said nothing, and his lawyer did not cross-examine any of the prosecution witnesses. Mr Parkin, however, said a great deal and put forward an unexpected defence. He denied that he had been in the house at all – the police, he said, were simply lying about this. He agreed, however, that he had been in the vicinity of this house in the hours of darkness, but that was because he had gone there simply to engage in what he regarded as 'perfectly innocent' poaching. The police had arrested him on the banks of the Tweed outside the house, he said, having allowed the real housebreakers to get away under their very noses. And he maintained that since the police could not possibly return empty-handed to their police station after their tip-off and their setting up this watch for housebreakers, they had arrested him and his poaching companion and charged them with housebreaking simply to save face with their colleagues and superiors.

There are no limits to what an accused person or his optimistic lawyer will ask a jury to believe, but this was much too much for the jury. Quite apart from the fact that there was no evidence of poaching equipment having been there, and the fact that he got no support from his companion, it strained credulity to accept, as Mr Parkin would have the jury do, that while he and his companion were unlawfully operating outside this isolated house, two other persons were quite coincidentally operating unlawfully inside it.

The two accused were duly convicted, and I sentenced Mr Parkin to two years' imprisonment. He was quite an engaging old rogue, and my heart further warmed to him when some weeks later I received a letter from him. In it he complained that he had read in the press that I had sentenced a sex offender to one year's imprisonment, while he himself had been sentenced to twice that amount. His letter finished in heroic fashion: 'You're probably a pervert yourself, you senile old fool.'

Whipping is wanted

In October 1940 the Sheriff at Peebles (who was, incidentally, the father of Lord Justice Clerk Cullen) decided that it was high time that whipping, which had fallen into disuse, should again be available as a means of dealing with juvenile offenders. The Sheriff Principal agreed; so did the Honorary Sheriffs; and so did the procurator fiscal. As with many new or revived procedures, however, it was more easily decided upon than put into practice.

I discovered a remarkable tract of correspondence in the library of Peebles Sheriff Court which demonstrates the unhappy lot of the sheriff clerk in seeking to give effect to the Sheriffs' wishes. If they wanted to have whipping, then he would have to provide (a) a whip and (b) a whipper. From where was he going to get them, and who would pay for them? Had this been today and not 1940, there would have been no problem – Scottish Courts Administration would no doubt have effortlessly attended to everything. But in 1940 the sheriff clerk was on his own, and up against it.

A whipper is wanted

Writing to the Sheriff Principal on 16th October 1940, he said, 'I regret to say that the police have not been at all helpful and seem more concerned with putting obstacles in the way of the matter being considered than doing anything to help the court.' The sheriff clerk appeared to take the view that the police force was the natural source of assistance in this as in other matters, and was clearly aggrieved when the local superintendent declined to be involved in anything which might smack of police brutality unless he had the express consent of the chief constable. So the sheriff clerk took high constitutional ground and referred the Sheriff Principal to *County Council of Dumfries v Phyn* (1895) 22 R 538 as regards the bounden duty of the police vis-à-vis the courts. The Sheriff Principal must have been impressed by this authority, for, presumably with the Sheriff Principal's blessing, the sheriff clerk persevered with the police. His perseverance was rewarded; and the superintendent was eventually persuaded to detail one of his men to volunteer for appointment as whipper not only to the Sheriff Court at Peebles, but also to the Burgh Court of Peebles and to the Burgh Court of Innerleithen. On 23rd October, accordingly, Police War Reserve Alexander Somerville was duly appointed to this threefold office.

Whips are wanted

So far, so good. But a whipper needs must have a whip. Again the sheriff clerk found himself in the toils. Writing to the King's and Lord Treasurer's Remembrancer on 18th November 1940, he said: 'My difficulty here is that as new sets of birch rods and tawse will be required, no one here can give me any information as to who should give the necessary orders for the supply of these articles and against what authority or department is the same chargeable.' He regretted 'troubling you on this trifling matter', and added, 'I can get no information locally and the police here are far from helpful.' But was this not a little ungracious? Had not the police helped by nominating PC Somerville as whipper? And could he not have followed the example of the then newly formed Home Guard, who were improvising with makeshift weapons until the real things came along?

At any rate, the King's and Lord Treasurer's Remembrancer came to the rescue immediately. The very next day he wrote back to the sheriff clerk to say that 'as the expenses of whipping formed a charge against the police grant, the police authorities would appear to be responsible for the provision of new sets of birch rods and tawse'. Further comfort was given to the sheriff clerk by the advice to him to go right to the top and communicate with the Secretary of the Scottish Home Department if he had any further difficulty.

No doubt glowing with a perfect piety, the sheriff clerk at once wrote to the superintendent of police, quoting from this letter and asking him to be good enough therefore 'to give instructions for the supply of four birch rods and two sets of tawse'. Then, rubbing bureaucratic salt into the superintendent's wounds, he went on to say: 'As under the regulations no whipping instrument can be brought into use until the same has been seen and approved by the Sheriff, it will be necessary for the sets of birch rods and tawse to be approved and docquetted.' Poor superintendent! Not only did he have to find out where to buy the whipping instruments and pay for them, but he could not be trusted to buy the right things – they had to be lodged, approved and docquetted as approved! And how would the superintendent know whether Sheriff Cullen would approve? It might all be a waste of money.

But the sheriff clerk was not done yet. His letter ended on a high note: 'Owing to the increase in juvenile delinquency in this county it is highly desirable that the Sheriff's orders for reviving this method of punishment should be carried out with the least possible delay.' Again, poor superintendent! Drop everything – forget enforcement of the blackout and prevention of the black market – your first priority at this stage of the war is to do everything you can to ensure that bad boys can be birched!

Fees to be paid

The superintendent duly responded to the pressure from the sheriff clerk and procured the necessary instruments. All was at last set for the flagellation of youthful malefactors to be resumed in Peebles – and to be resumed by professionals, for, as with most legal services, there were fees to be paid. The Table of Fees for whippers of juvenile offenders was authorized by the Treasury in 1885, and provided *inter alia*:–

For whipping one offender	£0 2 6
For whipping on the same day,	
each additional offender	0 1 0
But not to exceed for a whole day,	
whatever the number whipped	0 10 0

And, with a pretty touch of wit, it was further provided that these fees would be charged against the prison vote as part of the necessary expense for 'the maintenance of a prisoner'. The inverted commas, it should be said, were also provided by the Treasury. No doubt fortified by this Table, PC Somerville was now ready, willing and able to maintain his prisoners.

After discovering this correspondence from 1940 I asked the procurator fiscal to instigate a search within his department's repositories; and there they were indeed found, the birch rods and the tawse. Furthermore, attached to the tawse was an OHMS label, and on it, in just decipherable writing, the word 'Approved' followed by the Sheriff's signature and the date 26/12/40. *Omnia rite ac solemniter acta erant!* (Everything had been done properly and in order!) The Sheriff had indeed docquetted his approval, although what criteria he had directed himself to apply must remain a matter for conjecture.

The whipper reappears

There, then, were the whips. But what use had been made of them, and what had become of the whipper? The Scottish Record Office searched diligently, but could find no trace of the Whipping Register which should have been lodged there when complete. Inquiry was thereafter made among the senior citizens of Peebles, and this revealed that Mr Somerville had emigrated to Australia in 1946. The trail appeared to have come to an end, but then, one day in April 1986, an elderly gentleman presented himself at my chambers in Peebles. It was indeed the whipper, Sandy Somerville, himself in person, returned on holiday from Australia, and, at the age of eighty-one, reporting for duty!

It was, of course, my melancholy duty to break the news to him that there would be no further call for his services, since whipping had long ago been abolished. The Table of Fees was mentioned, however, and inevitably the question was raised,

'How much did you make out of it?' More of this later. Then the question was asked, 'Were you ever discharged?'

The whipper is discharged

Since it turned out that he had not been discharged, and since he would be in Peebles during the town's Beltane Festival, it was felt appropriate that Mr Somerville should be discharged with fitting solemnity on the high day of this gala week. The ceremony duly took place on 21st June 1986. Earlier in the day the Chief Constable of the Lothians came to Peebles and congratulated him on his long record in office. Then at the Beltane lunch, in the presence of leading local citizens – the Cornet and his Lass, the Beltane Queen and her Courtiers, the Warden of Neidpath, the Warden of the Cross Kirk, the Convenor of the District Council, and the local Member of Parliament Sir David Steel – the procurator fiscal emeritus, Eddie Laverock, read out the terms of his discharge. All men were invited to know by those presents that whereas this, that and the next thing, whereas the said Alexander Somerville had faithfully held office as whipper for 45 years, 7 months and 29 days, and whereas, after another whereas or two, it appeared expedient that he be relieved of the care and burden of office, now therefore he was not only exonerated but also *simpliciter* discharged from the said office as from Beltane Saturday 1986. The incumbent procurator fiscal, Fergus Brown, then presented him with a tangible token of the town's gratitude for his services, and, not surprisingly, this turned out to be one of the birch rods – by kind permission of the police, in whom, by virtue of their having paid for it originally, the right of property in it had presumably vested.

Mr Somerville received this gift most graciously, gave it a nostalgic swish or two, and then made an excellent speech, concluding with four lines of verse which gave the answer to the 64,000 dollar question:–

> *In this room today I stand*
> *With this birch rod in my hand;*
> *On not one body was it ever laid,*
> *And never a penny was I ever paid.*

So the Sheriffs and Burgh Court magistrates had never made use of the disposal which the sheriff clerk had been at such pains to make available! Mr Somerville then went on to say that customs officers in Australia would be unlikely to allow his birch rod's entry into that country. And since he felt that the best thing he could do with it in these circumstances was to present it to the local community, he accordingly handed it over to the chairman of the District Council for safe keeping in the Peebles Museum. There, then, safely disarmed within its municipal silo – for woodworm had long since reduced to zero its first-strike capacity – the Peebles deterrent is now to be found. As a deterrent it had been extremely cost-effective. Its mere existence had obviously been sufficient: it had never had to be used, and there had been no revenue implications to the capital outlay upon it.

8

The Edinburgh Youth Orchestra

Our children's music

Our two children have given us great and sustained pleasure over the years. Our daughter Ingalo inherited her mother's gifts as a pianist and became an equally accomplished violinist as well. Her younger brother Diggi, no doubt put off by his sister's prowess, made little of either violin or piano, but became an equally accomplished solo recorder player. Ingalo became a team player as well as a soloist. She led her school orchestra, played in the National Youth Orchestra of Great Britain and in 1985 and 1986 was the leader of the Edinburgh Youth Orchestra, commonly known as the EYO.

The Easter course of the EYO

The EYO was founded in 1963 by the celebrated organist of St Giles Cathedral, Herrick Bunney. Under his chairmanship the orchestra rapidly developed to the present position it holds among the pre-eminent youth orchestras of the United Kingdom, and it regularly attracts far more applications for places than even an extended symphony orchestra can accommodate. The majority of the players belong to Edinburgh, but such is the orchestra's reputation that applications for audition come from many other parts of Great Britain. During the annual Easter course, over 100 talented young musicians between the ages of thirteen and twenty-one are trained by a conductor of international standing and a team of professional coaches, the course culminating in concerts out of town and in Edinburgh's Usher Hall. At other times of the year, string and wind groups from the EYO play at civic and charitable functions, but the Easter course is the centrepiece of its life and work.

Twelve successive Easters were dominated in our family life by the EYO, for Ingalo played in it for six years, and on her retiral as leader I was asked to become the chairman, and remained in the chair for the next six years. I enjoyed my time immensely as chairman. Players, their parents, conductors, coaches, board members – all formed part of an extended happy family, and its close-knit family feeling is indeed one of the great strengths of the EYO. Players come and go with the years, but the orchestra does not change – at least in the standards it sets itself. It is new every year and yet it is the same every year, a very gifted company of youngsters who are, in effect, Edinburgh's 'Young Musicians of the Year'. It was a great privilege to be involved with them.

The annual Easter course was a non-stop whirlwind affair. In my time it took place in George Watson's College, which had ample room in its great Assembly Hall for the full orchestra of 110 or so players and many classrooms where the individual sections of the orchestra could practise under the attentive eyes and ears of their coaches. Thus 1st violins practised in one room, 2nd violins in another, violas in a third and so on. The coaches were all professional exponents of their instruments, some of them full-time teachers, some of them full-time orchestral players. The course was strictly timetabled, with so many periods for sectional practice, so many for practice by all the strings or all the wind, and so many for the full orchestra.

A fine camaraderie developed among the players. Many were already known to each other, from school or from other orchestras or from previous years in the EYO. A Players Committee arranged dances and informal concerts – where musical hair was let down and party pieces performed. A Parents Committee arranged refreshments throughout the course. Members of the Board of Directors, which was formed of parents of players, former players, musicians and musically interested businessmen, took it in turns to supervise. But the two persons upon whom success ultimately depended were, of course, the conductor and the administrator.

There have been many conductors of the EYO, the most distinguished having been Sir Malcolm Arnold and James Loughran. In my time the conductors were Christopher Adey and Alexandre Myrat. Adey, an Englishman, was lean and cadaverous with a gravel voice that Humphrey Bogart would have recognized. Myrat, a Greek, was suave and smooth with a French accent that added to his charm. Both went down very well with the girls in the orchestra, particularly Adey.

The administrator's work was endless. It went on all year round, arranging auditions, engaging coaches, organizing fundraising, producing programme notes, arranging concerts by small groups throughout the year, by the full orchestra at Easter time, and then running the whole Easter course; and if there was to be a tour, then of course the burden of administrative work was more than doubled. The two administrators with whom I worked were very different in their approach to things, but both very effective. Fiona Donaldson, a former member of the orchestra, was at the heart of musical life in Edinburgh, working in the University's music department where she organized the University's year-round lunchtime concerts; and being a double bass player she was much in demand for the many *ad hoc* orchestras which Edinburgh's musical life requires. Her successor Marjory Dougall had had two children in the orchestra and brought a school teacher's insight into the workings of the adolescent mind as well as that of a parent. She had much creative imagination, well exemplified in her first incursion into fundraising for the orchestra; five works by composers of different nationalities were to be played at the Easter concert, and she persuaded five Edinburgh restaurants of the same nationalities as the composers to sponsor the appropriate works.

The Silver Jubilee tour to California

1988 saw the start of the EYO's twenty-fifth year. One of Edinburgh's twin towns is San Diego, and its youth orchestra had come to play at the 1987 Edinburgh Festival of Youth Orchestras. Contact was of course made with them and they politely invited the EYO to visit San Diego. So it was decided to take them at their word, and to make a tour of California in the summer of 1989 the climax of the Silver Jubilee celebrations.

This was a tremendous undertaking, and, looking back, I wonder if we would have embarked upon it if we had known all that it would involve. But thank goodness we did, for it was also huge fun and quite unforgettable. Work before play, however, and there was the little matter of £40,000 to be raised in order to reduce the cost of the tour to a reasonable amount for players or, more accurately, their parents. The overall cost was of course greatly reduced by the kind offer made by the youth orchestras of the various places we proposed to visit to provide private hospitality for our party. This was one of the best features of the tour, for our youngsters had the opportunity to stay in the homes of their counterparts in the American orchestras, and to experience at first hand what they had so often seen on the movies of the American way of life.

But flights, internal travel, university hostels at the beginning and end of the tour, and conductor's and coaches' fees all had to be taken into account, and the total budget was a high one. What, then, would be a reasonable amount for the individual player's parent to pay? We realized that most parents had become used to paying for annual school trips abroad – on straightforward exchanges, for example, or on skiing holidays – and took the view that the California tour should be looked upon as the trip of a lifetime, worth two such 'normal' trips. So the cost was fixed at approximately double the cost of a school skiing holiday, with special arrangements being made for those with more than one child in the orchestra or known to be in reduced circumstances.

Fundraising for the tour

I was glad that I had had the experience of raising funds for the Strathaven Town Mill project. Here, however, the emphasis had to be on private funding, because the only public funding bodies which would be relevant were the local education authorities, and by this time their funds for this sort of thing had largely dried up. So a long list of charitable trusts and commercial companies was prepared, and I approached them on what I thought of as the Polyfoto principle. Polyfoto was the name of the chain of photographic shops up and down the land that flourished in the 1940s and 50s, where you sat in a chair and forty-eight different photographs were taken of you. You could change your expression, your 'angle of attack' and even your hat as much as you liked. And they had a marvellous advertising slogan – 'One of the 48 *must* be good!' So with fundraising. For every forty-eight begging letters you sent out, one usually brought a favourable response.

But it was a time-consuming business. You had to find out who was the appropriate person to write to, whether chairman, managing director, secretary or PR person, and also his or her name, so that a letter could be written and addressed on a personal basis. Charitable Trusts were obviously the better bet, for their whole *raison d'être* was to hand out money; but of course you had to ensure that the trusts you approached were entitled to support music or young people or education. Commercial companies have no obligation to support anyone other than their shareholders, but many do support charitable causes, not only out of the goodness of their corporate heart but also in the interests of their public relations – which consideration I had to stress (shamelessly) in my letters to them.

However, if one of the forty-eight were good just on the basis of a letter, the other forty-seven would require a follow-up phone call if there was to be any prospect of a favourable response. I remember one particularly honest response. I enquired of the managing director on the phone if he had received my letter, and he cheerfully replied, 'Yes, and I put it straight in the bin.' Most letters were at least acknowledged with that same message, although phrased in less direct terms; and this, of course, was in no way surprising since most companies are deluged with charitable appeals all the time. Their replies, however, had to be carefully read between the lines as well as on the lines in order to see whether their entries on the list should be marked 'No good' or 'Try again later'.

Fundraising functions of many sorts took place. The players were issued with family swear-boxes in the form of margarine tubs bearing the message 'With every penny in the drum, California here I come'; they were encouraged to organize their own small-scale concerts in their own homes, and to take part in the 24-hour non-stop concert by the full orchestra in the Queen's Hall. Now this was a remarkable happening. Starting at nine o'clock at night, the orchestra did indeed play all through the night and on till nine o'clock the next night. Players came and went – they were sponsored for how many hours they could continue, and at least one player actually did play throughout the whole twenty-four hours. Conductors came and went also, and the public at large were offered the chance not only to listen to the music but – for a suitable donation – to conduct the orchestra themselves. The Lord Provost, Eleanor Mclachlan, was one of the first-time conductors, taking the orchestra through a spirited rendition of the overture to Glinka's *Ruslan and Lyudmila*. I took it upon myself to conduct the last piece – the orchestra took me through it rather than I them – which was 'The Seven Hills March'. This we had commissioned from the distinguished Scottish composer Neil Butterworth, who was the father of the then leader of the orchestra.

The Seven Hills March

This composition had an unusual provenance. I had had a case in court relating to a brochure advertising a hotel, and part of the text of the brochure read 'Like its sister city Athens, Edinburgh is built on seven hills'. Here, however, two things were confused. Edinburgh used to be known as 'Modern Athens', but it was Rome, not Athens, which, like Edinburgh, is built on seven hills. None the less, the idea of Edinburgh's seven hills stuck in my mind, and I eventually had the idea of having an open-air concert where one section of the orchestra would go to the top of one of the hills, another section to the top of another hill and so on, the aim being to play their separate parts of the same piece at the same time. Each hill-top's music would be recorded, and all seven recorded parts put together to form a unique whole. Because of the difficulty of finding a suitable work, Neil Butterworth was commissioned to compose a special piece for the occasion, orchestrated in such a way that many of the parts were interchangeable among different instruments.

In order that all the parts would start together and finish together, a master recording of the piece played by the whole orchestra together under one conductor – the composer – was made; each hill-top section conductor was to listen to a copy of it in a Walkman as he conducted his section through the piece, with a view to finishing at exactly the same time as the master tape finished. It was thus not really necessary for all the sections to start together, which was just as well – for the nominal start time was the firing of the one o'clock gun from Edinburgh Castle, which would obviously be heard by the section on Castle Hill before anyone else.

There was some discussion as to just which were Edinburgh's seven hills. Castle Hill, Calton Hill, Blackford Hill and Arthur's Seat were obvious choices, and we eventually settled for the other three as being the Braid Hills, Craiglockhart Hill and Corstorphine Hill. Since the players would have to be taken by car from their headquarters to their hills, sponsorship was sought from leading Edinburgh motor dealers. This was relatively easily obtained after it was discovered that the daughter of one of the dealers was the girlfriend of one of our brass players, and the good example of this dealer's ready and generous sponsorship could be quoted *pour encourager les autres.*

On the appointed day all gathered in the Reid Hall. Neil Butterworth had composed a stirring piece, and after it had been recorded and seven copies of it made for the seven hill-top section conductors, seven happy carloads of players were driven off to the seven hills. It was a fine sight to see! They were going off to take part in what must surely have been a unique world premiere – the first time a new composition had had its first public performance over an area of fifteen square miles and up to 800 feet in height. The countdown to one o'clock over, the gun duly fired and the players were off. Audiences varied in size, from amazed tourists at the Castle and startled joggers on Arthur's Seat to unconcerned sheep on the Braids. But alas and alack! The grand design of making a composite recording from the seven separate recordings could not succeed – for although each hill-top conductor listened to the master recording (three minutes and twenty seconds long) as he conducted, the seven separate recordings varied in length from three minutes fifteen seconds to four minutes four seconds!

'Off to California in the morning'

If faith in recording technology had not been realized, faith otherwise was well rewarded. Arranging the tour had been a great act of faith. Faith that sufficient funds could be raised to reduce to a tolerable level the cost which individual parents would have to bear; faith that sufficient numbers of players from each section of the orchestra would wish to tour, and faith that the staggering logistics – of arranging seven concerts, of transporting the orchestra and its instruments to, from and within California, and of finding accommodation for the whole party – could be overcome. But faith accompanied by works 'achieveth much', and two years of preparation were rewarded by a farewell reception by the Lord Provost in the City Chambers and a wholly happy and successful three weeks in California.

The party consisted of 101 players, one conductor, one soloist, three professional coaches and twelve supervising adults. For many of the youngsters it was a first journey by air. The Jumbo Jet awaiting them on the tarmac at Prestwick looked like a huge white horizontal skyscraper, but once up and away, the joys of airborne meals and in-flight movies allayed any apprehension they might have had. Landfall was in New York, then Detroit, and at last San Diego.

There, then, was the land that had been promised for two years, never quite seeming to be more than a dream, but now a stunning reality. We had lost count of time. Someone said it was twenty-four hours since we had piled into buses, half a world away at Watson's College; someone else said it was like the end of summertime only more so – you put the clock back not just one hour but eight. Whatever time it was, the only thing to do was to fall fast asleep in one of the student residences of San Diego State University.

Next morning we learnt what 'sunup' meant. The temperature crept up into the nineties, and stayed there relentlessly. The orchestra rested and recovered, helped by a swimming pool, a superabundance of ice cubes, an air-conditioned rehearsal hall, and the blessed discovery that all the instruments had survived the journey. It was July 4th, Independence Day, and after sundown, for the sun did at last go down, the sunburnt party went to Coronado to watch the most star-spangled fireworks display that they had ever seen.

Standing ovations

Acclimatized, retuned and re-rehearsed, the EYO travelled to Oceanside, some forty miles to the north of San Diego, for its first concert. It was a huge success. In a beautiful hall and to an audience of 400, the orchestra began its programme with *Golden City*, the fantasy-overture which we had commissioned for our Silver Jubilee from my former Arts Council colleague David Dorward. This was followed by the Max Bruch violin concerto, the soloist being Edward Dusinberre, a recent leader of the National Youth Orchestra of Great Britain. Then came Tchaikovsky's *Swan Lake* and Stravinsky's *Firebird* – and a standing ovation!

San Diego's Symphony Hall is one of the great concert halls of the world, and it was a moving experience to see and hear Edinburgh's young musicians of the year playing in such a majestic setting. Rachmaninov's Symphony No. 2 lasts a whole hour, but the passage of time went unnoticed; such was the compelling maturity of the orchestra's playing that the American audience again rose to its feet in a standing ovation. The average age of the players was only seventeen, yet the music critic of the *Los Angeles Times* went so far as to say: 'Smooth, sweet-toned and completely integrated, the timbre of the strings displayed the elegance of a Rolls-Royce Silver Cloud. Not a few professional American orchestras could find something to envy in the Edinburgh string sound.'

If the audiences were amazed at what they heard at the concerts, the players were amazed at what they saw on their days off. They had an absorbing morning at the world-famous San Diego Zoo, and an even more absorbing day at the marine circus, Sea World. The star performer there was a baby whale called Shamu, but the EYO's brass players performed there as well, and received a certificate attesting that 'they had made a big splash in Shamu's Musical Revue'. Then there were the cadillacs on the ten-lane freeways, the adobe mission buildings, the bougainvillea, the lemon trees and palm trees, the complete absence of litter on the streets, and the constant courtesy in the shops. Best of all was the hospitality in the homes of their opposite numbers, the members of the San Diego Youth Symphony. Here was the real heart of the tour in educational terms – a great exchange of young people's ideas about the world in general and music in particular.

The third concert at San Diego was given in the Casa del Prado theatre on a Sunday afternoon. This was probably the only time in its 25-year history that the EYO has had to turn away people who wanted to hear them. With eventually standing room only, it was a sell-out – but possibly because admission was free! The audience again stood to acknowledge the superlative performance which conductor Christopher Adey had won from the EYO. He had a remarkable rapport with the players. No fudge, no fuss, no need to shout or to cajole – he simply told them precisely what he wanted from them, and he got it. His acclaim as the leading conductor of youth orchestras is well deserved.

'Do you know the way to San Jose?' This songwriter's question was echoed by the EYO when it set off on a 500-mile drive northwards from San Diego in a caravan consisting of three buses, an instrument van and a car containing the conductor and administrator. The party was gathered-in to private homestays by the San Jose Youth Symphony, and again friendships were made and return visits pencilled-in. Concerts were given at San Jose State University, and in the magnificent Flint Centre at Cupertino. By this time we had come to realize that standing ovations for youth orchestras – unknown in Scotland – were standard practice in America, so we did not set too much store by them; still, it was very nice to receive them.

San Francisco

We had a marvellous day out in San Francisco, and could see at once how easy it had been for Tony Bennett to leave his heart there. Things that we had long heard about were all there to be seen for real – the Golden Gate bridge, Alcatraz, the cable cars, Pier 39 and Chinatown. A lot of time on the tour was spent by the adults in simply counting heads – were the youngsters still all there? – and nowhere was more counting done than in Chinatown. *Mirabile dictu*, all returned present and correct.

The Royal Bank of Scotland had been looking after our money requirements, and I had occasion to call at their offices there. Their address was the Pyramid Building, which turned out to be a magnificent slender pyramid of a skyscraper, and I thought to myself how well the Bank had done to acquire such an impressive home. But I had got it wrong. The Bank's home was simply two rooms on the thirty-seventh floor …

Disneyland

Next stop was Monterey for our last concert, which took place in the Robert Louis Stevenson school, and was followed by a beach party at Carmel and a glimpse of Pebble Beach Golf Course. Finally, work done, the EYO could relax at Disneyland before flying home from Los Angeles. What an extraordinary experience was that provided by The Mouse! Theme park to end all theme parks, high noon of hokum, ride after magical ride into adventureland, frontierland, fantasyland and all the other theme-parklands that stemmed from a creative imagination of probably infinite dimensions. Those of us who had gone there to scoff remained to pray. It was all done to such a high standard, and all so spotlessly clean. And when darkness fell and the final electric parade took place down Main Street, culminating in a float bearing Mickey and Minnie with their inner cabinet of Donald, Goofy and Pluto, all disbelief was suspended; Mickey and Minnie waved happily at us, and everyone of us waved happily back.

We got back home safely. Everyone had survived three hectic weeks, thanks to our generously open-hearted American hosts, our tour doctor Pamela Walker, who was a third-year medical student when not being the leader of our trumpet section, our indefatigable administrator Fiona Donaldson and our treasurer Michael Pentland, who fearlessly drove into the Los Angeles traffic nightmare to find the British consulate for a player's replacement passport. They did all the work, I just did the talking, but as the buck had to stop somewhere I was mightily relieved when we finally debussed in Edinburgh all present and correct.

With a song in my heart

A few weeks later, but I do not think *post hoc ergo propter hoc* (after this therefore because of this), I suffered a heart attack. A bypass operation was performed, but I understand that as I was wheeled out of the theatre the bells rang for panic stations and I was wheeled back in. All those neat stitches had to be unstitched, another vein located, and the operation performed all over again. With a spaghetti junction of wires and tubes going in and out of me, I must have looked like part of Dr Frankenstein's work-in-progress. At any rate, and as a result, I was in intensive care for nine days, and unconscious for four. Nobody, not even Lolo, could 'get through to me'. Then Lolo discovered that there was a fellow Icelander who was a nurse in the ward, and she asked her to speak to me in Icelandic to see if that would produce any reaction. Apparently it certainly did! I was told later that I had jumped up in alarm, no doubt because I had not 'switched on my Icelandic channel'. So I relapsed into unconsciousness. What eventually brought me round, though, was moving and beautiful. It was Lolo singing to me, and what she sang was one of my own songs – 'My Intended'.

9

Faith, Hope and Charity

Church service

At the outset of these memoirs I referred to my manse upbringing and to my original intention to enter the ministry myself. But though in due course I found I had to abandon this intention, I hoped I could be of some service to the church in other ways. In 1968 I accepted an invitation to become an assessor on the newly formed Church of Scotland's Selection Board for candidates for the ministry. I did so if only to put my own experience to some possible good use – because part of the selection process was to try to assess the candidates' commitment to their perceived vocation. My qualification for being on the board, accordingly, was that I had failed myself as a candidate through lack of sufficient commitment.

Selection Boards

It was a remarkable experience being on this board. Under the overall direction of the enchanting Dr Murdo Ewan Macdonald, the selection schools sat for three days at a time, with groups of three assessors dealing with groups of six candidates each. The whole process was based on the Civil Service selection procedure which in turn had been based on the War Office Selection Boards for officers. I had been through the latter procedure myself, and found it the most harrowing process I was ever subjected to – batteries of intelligence and personality tests, group discussions and group tasks with no one in charge (in order to see who emerged as natural leaders), physical agility and initiative tests, self-assessment and interviews culminating in the perplexing question 'Why do you want to become an officer?' What made it the more stressful was that when I went through the process towards the end of the war, when the demand for officers was greatly reduced, it was well known that the pass rate was a mere 30 per cent.

But in the Church of Scotland Selection Board it was, of course, at least hoped that the pass rate would be 100 per cent. Candidates knew this and so were less stressed, but still found it a very anxious-making experience. Apart from the physical element it was very similar to the army selection procedure, but it had two tests which the army did not have – one a committee test in which a group of candidates took it in turn to be chairman of a committee, and were assessed both on their performance as chairman and as committee member; and the other a 'tactful letter' test. Here they were given a rude letter from a church member relating to some aspect of congregational life, to which, as minister, they had to write an appropriate letter in reply. One test which *had* been included in the army process was for the candidates to say which of their fellow candidates they would like to have as their officer; and I regretted that the church candidates were not asked to say which of their fellow candidates they would like to have as their own minister. But I always asked myself which of them would be the best minister for me.

The candidates had three sets of interviews, with the Director, with a psychologist, and with a minister and layman together. It was here, as one of the lay assessors, that the process became particularly interesting for me. How firm was their belief? How far was their unbelief capable of being helped? Would they be effective salesmen? Could they really preach Christ and Him crucified? It was all designed to be a humane exercise – to try to spot those for whom the ministry would be unsuitable and stop them from proceeding further, so as to spare them from the misery of starting work as a minister and then, realizing that their level of commitment was inadequate, having to give up.

I found it all humbling and fascinating, particularly the final sessions of the schools when all the assessors pooled their impressions of the candidates, whether they had directly interviewed them or not. During the ten years from 1968 that I acted as an assessor, once or twice a year, most candidates were young students, few were 'evangelicals' and most of them were successful. There has apparently been a great change in recent years. More and more candidates are older, seeking a second career, many more evangelicals put themselves forward, and the pass rate has significantly declined. But for all those who are accepted and go on to become ordained ministers, I have nothing but the highest admiration.

The other Director with whom I worked was my own minister, the Very Rev Dr W.J.G. McDonald. Bill McDonald could be described as a textbook model of what a minister should be. He is immediately recognizable as a saint, immediately recognizable as a first-class academic, and immediately recognizable as a man who knows all about the world and his wife. Nothing could have been less surprising than that he should have been appointed Moderator of the 1989 General Assembly. In that office, incidentally, he followed a year or two after the Very Rev Professor James Whyte, whom he had already followed as Dux of Stewart's College, and had immediately followed as minister of Mayfield!

Sunday School lessons

Bill McDonald, who became one of my close friends, had asked me years before to become the superintendent of his Sunday School, and I acted in this capacity for six happy years until we left Edinburgh for Strathaven. There had been some dissatisfaction with the teaching material then in use, and during my time as superintendent I particularly enjoyed leading a committee which compiled a six-year course of teaching to replace it. I read through all the teaching material used in the various denominations of the Christian church, and found this very illuminating. The Church of Scotland Sunday School material at that time consisted of 90 per cent what might be called 'bible stories' and perhaps 10 per cent doctrinal theology. In the Roman Catholic Church it was exactly the other way round – 90 per cent doctrine and only 10 per cent bible stories. I have sometimes thought that the glory of the Catholic Church is that the doctrine is all cut and dried, and you just sign on the dotted line, while the shame is that you are not allowed to think for yourself. The glory of the Church of Scotland is that you are allowed to think for yourself; the shame is that few people do so.

So I felt that there should be more emphasis on doctrine in our Sunday School course. After all, there are normally two sides to any religion – its metaphysics and its ethics. There is not a great deal of difference between the ethical positions of the great religions, but Christian metaphysics are distinct, and difficult, and, so far as they are capable of explanation, need to be taught. Eventually a course was put together which made much use of Anglican and Methodist material but otherwise was home-made. My last job in the army had been with a travelling wing of instructors, and I made much use of the Army's manual of instruction, which among other things laid stress on the preparation of a lesson plan, showing exactly where audio and visual aids should be used in the course of the lesson, and we greatly enjoyed constructing an Army-style sand-table model for use in teaching Old Testament history. I was not ready for what might be called the jet age in Sunday Schools where you just take the children skiing; our course was more piston-engined and firmly bible-based.

George MacLeod

It is not too fanciful to suggest that the jet age in the Church of Scotland as a whole arrived with the Iona Community. Once regarded as the red guards of the Church of Scotland, the community is now fully within the church's fold. I have a great respect for it, and had the immense privilege of working under its founder, the legendary George MacLeod, at his summer camps on Iona. I regard him as having been one of the three great church leaders in Scotland, the other two in my estimation being John Knox and Thomas Chalmers. As leaders of the young people's camps we were expected to work with him and call him 'George', but I could not bring myself to do this. He looked every inch the very model of a modern major-general, and while I was wholly happy to work *under* him as a young subaltern, I thought it would have been presumptuous to think of working *with* him and calling him 'George'. I much preferred to call him 'Sir'. He was, as it happened, a baronet, but combined a patrician appearance and manner with a passionate concern for the underclass. He was a marvellous preacher, being able to reconcile very persuasively the eventual mystery of God with the immediate presence of God; and the deep spirituality of his praying and preaching was embodied in his insistence on making religion wholly relevant to modern industrial life. Not everyone in the Church of Scotland agreed with him, but love him or not, his tremendous personality was unforgettable. I loved him and was only sorry that I could not feel more at ease in his presence.

The Church of Scotland

On returning to Edinburgh from Strathaven, I decided to take a 'sabbatical' from church membership, and spent a most interesting year visiting all sorts of places of worship, from the Tridentine Mass at one extreme to the Quaker meeting at the other extreme. My experience of the outlawed Tridentine mass (i.e. the traditional mass in Latin) was a disappointment, however. It was conducted in a back room of the Churchill Theatre by a priest from New Zealand. I had been looking forward to following the majestic Latin which for centuries had been heard in Catholic churches throughout the world, but unfortunately the priest knelt with his back to the congregation and spoke so rapidly that all I could make out was that he was speaking Latin with a pronounced New Zealand accent!

Of all the places of worship I went to, undoubtedly the warmest welcome came from the Quaker meeting – which was as it should be, since their formal title is 'The Religious Society of Friends'. (That said, just sitting silently for an hour was hard work.) Home is where you start from, however, and at the end of the year I came back home to the Church of Scotland.

The British Association for Counselling

Sickness in mind and body is one of the great problems with which mankind has to wrestle. I was struck long ago with the saying that good mental hygiene requires that one should have a confidant, and time and again in court it appeared that what the offender required was not so much punishment as just someone to whom he could talk and who would listen to him. Often enough there had been no one to listen to him. No one had wanted him, no one had appreciated him. He could not work out his own problems. He felt he was a non-person. Herein lay the value of probation – for the supervising social worker was expected to advise, guide and befriend. The really effective ones were those who could help their probationers work out the answers to their problems themselves. In so doing, such social workers were acting as counsellors in the proper sense of the term as it is now understood – not giving advice or counsel, but helping the troubled mind find its own good advice itself.

One of the psychologists with whom I had worked on the Church of Scotland Selection Boards founded the Scottish Association for Counselling, and asked me to be one of its vice-presidents. Although I was not myself a counsellor, I was glad to be associated with this body, and after it had been dissolved, as a vice-president of the British Association for Counselling. Now the process of counselling or psychotherapy has not always had a good press, and has been the butt of many jokes ('Everyone in California,' I was told when there with the EYO, 'is either in therapy or is a therapist or is a therapist in therapy.'). But oh, how important it is that those who need psychotherapy should be able to get it! Many patients go to their GPs just to have a talk, but what can a GP do in the standard six-minute consultation? What I would like to see in the fullness of time is a team of counsellors attached to each doctor's practice, so that the doctor could refer to them those patients whose underlying trouble is an unquiet mind, whatever the surface physical symptoms may be. At any rate, the British Association for Counselling is now a flourishing body with some 17,000 members seeking to make life happier for those who come to see them or are referred to them by GPs or otherwise.

Tenovus-Scotland

I was also involved with a body primarily concerned with bodily health, the medical research charity called Tenovus. This sounds like a Latin word, but isn't. The charity had been started in Cardiff by ten men who had had good reason to be grateful to medical science and wanted to do something for it in return. Casting about for a name, they went no further than the fact that there were ten of them round the table, and settled for Tenovus. In 1977 the name was brought to Scotland by one of the most distinguished surgeons which Scotland has ever known,

Sir Charles Illingworth. Quick-silver, dapper, peppery, droll, old-world, he was nevertheless a man of tireless energy, who set up in retirement a charity to promote medical research, now organized throughout the land, under the name of Tenovus-Scotland. Its scope is wide, and it promotes research into any medical aspect of the human condition, bridging the gap in funding between what is required and what can be provided by Government and University funds. All of the research which it promotes is carried out in Scotland.

Now most of the spectacular life-threatening conditions have their own dedicated research charities, such as the Imperial Cancer Research Fund or the British Heart Foundation; but what I liked about Tenovus was that it was just as prepared to put money into research into other conditions that do not command public attention in the same way but require just as much research. A project which would be eminently suitable for Tenovus to support would thus be research into teenage acne. Not a life-threatening condition, clearly, but it must cause great distress to those who suffer from it. There is no Imperial Teenage Acne Fund or British Acne Foundation, and I was sorry that no dermatologist came forward with a project for such research during my time with Tenovus.

I was chairman of the Lanarkshire Committee and then the Edinburgh Committee. These committees received proposals for research, decided whether or not to support them, and passed on to the central scientific advisory committee those which they did decide to support. If the latter committee gave its approval, then the local committee set about raising funds to meet the cost of the research.

Fundraising! This had been a major village industry in Strathaven, and at times I got my lines crossed as I found myself involved in raising funds for Tenovus, for the Town Mill and for the East Church bicentenary all at the same time. Strathaven was the land of the perpetual coffee morning and the endless jumble sale – sometimes it seemed as if the same collection of jumble appeared and reappeared at each successive sale. Tenovus took higher ground, however, with fundraisers such as dinners (menus in Latin), golf tournaments, concerts in the Usher Hall, fashion shows, and Burns Suppers in the Signet Library.

It all proceeded on the basis that disease is there and shouldn't be there, while money for medical research isn't there and should be there. Disease was always looked upon as an intruder, and while it is still with us in this generation, the research done today will seek to keep the intruder at bay for future generations. Tenovus has accordingly supported research into, among other things, hypothermia, migraine, slipped discs, osteoporosis and cot deaths; and has helped to develop mobile intensive care units and the 'trans-rectal probe for carcinoma of the prostate', to give the official title to what is affectionately known to those who work with it as the 'bum-gun'.

Everything in Tenovus was done in tens. So after ten years' service as a regional chairman, I retired in 1983.

The Council for Music in Hospitals

My interest in the relief of suffering and my interest in music were combined in my last out-of-court activity – the Council for Music in Hospitals. This has nothing to do with bedside radios in the wards of general hospitals. What the Council does is to provide live concerts in hospitals by professional musicians, and does so for two reasons – first, to bring musical entertainment to those who cannot go out to enjoy it, and secondly, to assist in the healing process. If laughter is the best medicine, music is not far behind, and its therapeutic value is well recognized.

The musicians are selected at auditions not just for their technical ability as performers, but for their caring potential as communicators. Just as a doctor requires to have a good 'bedside manner', so do our musicians. It is principally in geriatric and psychiatric hospitals that they perform, as well as in hospices and homes, and the ability to take a patient's hand and hold it while singing to him or to dance with a patient while another musician plays, and in all circumstances to smile happily at the audience, is of great importance. By far the most popular music are the songs the patients were brought up on – wartime songs and songs from the shows – and it is a wonderful experience to see faces which were dull and stone-like to begin with gradually relax, soften and finally smile with tears not far away as songs they heard their mothers sing are heard again. It is by no means uncommon to hear of the delighted astonishment of nurses when they hear a stroke patient, up till then without speech, suddenly break into song. Feedback is sought after every concert, and time and again reports say things like, 'The artists immediately made us feel we were all old friends. A wonderful range of items; the audience loved it – spontaneous appreciation, feet tapping, joining in the songs and calling for more.' Or 'You could see by the expression on their faces – they felt special' and 'I wish we could have a concert every week.'

It all began in Scotland in 1980, when a marvellous lady called Nella Kerr was asked by the Director of the Council in England (which had already been on the go for thirty years) to start up a separate organization here. She had to find musicians willing to perform for fees of about half the commercial rate. She had to find hospitals and homes willing and able to buy concerts from her. She had to find patrons and committee members. She had to raise funds to meet the shortfall between the cost of the concerts and the amount which the hospitals and homes could pay for them. And she had to recruit staff to assist her in the ever expanding work involved. All this she did, and did it so successfully that when she retired in 1996 the number of concerts presented that year was no less than 1690. Her admirable successor Alison Frazer has maintained this momentum by achieving 2000 concerts in the year 2000, and their work has brought unmeasurable comfort and joy to the sick, the disturbed and the old throughout Scotland. It has been my privilege to have been the chairman of the Scottish committee since 1991, and to have worked not only with these ladies, but also with the Council's former United Kingdom President, Ian Wallace. Ian is of course the much-loved Scottish entertainer known to millions through the radio programme *My Music*, and is probably the only artist to have been a star of grand opera, comic opera and soap opera – having played the part of the vet in *Take the High Road*.

Little Sister

Forty years ago I wrote a musical romance called *Little Sister*. It was centred on the concert that Chopin gave in Edinburgh in 1848. Romance has to have a barrier between hero and heroine which requires to be broken down, and my original idea was that the barrier between the hero and heroine was a psychological one which would be resolved by their mutual involvement in Chopin's music. Having thought about this for a long time and got nowhere with it, I then remembered a piece of advice from an old family doctor we once had. When he had patients who believed they were suffering from complicated conditions he would say to them, 'Why not think of something simple? – it usually is!' So I thought of something much simpler by way of barrier and resolution – the heroine hadn't been able to get a ticket for Chopin's concert and blamed the hero; so he not only got her a ticket but arranged for her to meet Chopin himself. As soon as this simple scenario occurred to me, the play more or less wrote itself in three weeks. I had composed most of the songs over the years. Their lyrics required some adjustment to fit into the play but otherwise only two or three more songs were required. One, 'The Green Loch', I made up coming home to Edinburgh on the Glasgow train; it started as a quick waltz in a major key at Queen Street, but had become a slow waltz in a minor key by the time the train got to Waverley. Another, 'Look in the looking-glass', came to me as I was having a shower in the many mirrored bathroom of a motel in central Sweden.

I had never intended that the play should be staged – I only hoped to have some evenings when friends could come round to read a part and recordings of the music could be switched on at the appropriate moments. But in 1993 I realized that if I could resurrect the Harpic Players from my Bar days I could put the show on as a fundraiser for the Council for Music in Hospitals. A quorum of the Harpics readily resurrected themselves, but in view of the fact that their average age was seventy-one, for Cameron Miller had turned eighty and Lionel Daiches was eighty-two, two departures from normal stage conventions were made: one was the convention that actors memorize their lines, the other that characters in a musical play sing the songs allotted to their part. What we did was that when it came to the time for a character to sing a song, he simply sat down and a youthful singer came forward and sang the song in his place; otherwise the actors acted their parts normally, but simply kept their scripts in their hands. This had two great advantages. It meant that we could get away with only two rehearsals, and that the perennial problem for amateur actors of what to do with their hands was solved – they had to hold on to their scripts. And after ten minutes the audience stopped noticing. A salon orchestra played, a double quartet sang, and the Harpics once again lived up to their cherished motto 'Our best is not too good'. It was all great fun, and raised a lot of money for Music in Hospitals.

Coda

The law is said to be an ass, but music, when soft voices die, lingers in the memory. Such law as once I knew will linger in my memory less long than the music, but being involved in both has been a wonderful privilege for me. 'Give me the making of the songs of a nation,' said Andrew Fletcher in 1703, 'and I care not who makes its laws.' With that I respectfully agree, and, as the supporting judges in the Appeal Court often used to say, 'there is nothing I can usefully add.'

Appendix One

The Sentence of the Court

The Art of Sentencing

It has been said that 'Sentencing is the most delicate, difficult and distasteful task for a judge'. I agree wholeheartedly. Sentencing is not made any easier by the knowledge that whatever sentence you impose, it is bound to be wrong from somebody's point of view. Different voices outside the legal profession speak continually on the subject, ranging at one extreme from do-gooders saying 'They're all sick, love them' to do-badders at the other extreme saying 'They're all wicked, flog them'. And it is not made any easier by the lack of attention paid to sentencing within the legal profession other than by the High Court. Indeed, the eminent criminologist Professor Nigel Walker has said that 'if the criminal law is the Cinderella of jurisprudence, then sentencing is Cinderella's illegitimate baby.' How, I wonder, can the baby's status be improved?

Two things are not always appreciated by the public. First, that sentencing is an art, not a science. It could, of course, be made into a science, as it appears to be in some other countries – a precise tariff is prescribed by law, including specific additions for aggravating factors and detailed deductions for mitigating factors: the Sheriff would then simply press the appropriate keys on his computer, and its penal cash register would ring up the net total of the sentence. Such a system would have the advantage of certainty, but it might well add up to injustice in many cases. It is quite contrary to the Scottish system, which, within prescribed limits, leaves sentencing as a matter for the judge's discretion. This, I believe, is as it ought to be, for the circumstances of one crime and one criminal are never the same as another.

Punishment should fit both the crime and the criminal. I made it a practice not to criticise other judges' sentences because I had not sat in their court when they came to pass those sentences – I had not heard all the facts that they had heard, and I had not experienced the offender that they had had before them. And I have little time for those who do criticise sentences, simply because the criticism is so often uninformed: the newspaper which the critic read will not have reported the full circumstances which the evidence disclosed in court about the crime, and this same critic will certainly not have experienced the convicted man face-to-face in court as the sentencer will have done. Sentencing is, if you like, a personal confrontation between one individual and another. Both persons are unique individuals – the judge will have *his* particular personality, outlook and attitudes, the offender will also have his particular personality, outlook and attitudes. If the judge is entitled to expect to receive respect in court, so too should the offender be entitled to receive at least the respect of being treated as an individual.

The second thing not always appreciated by the public is that although penology has come a long way in the last 100 years, it remains in its relative infancy. We still do not know particularly much about what makes people tick, but the more we learn about human behaviour the better will we be able to know in the future what to do with the offenders in our midst. We have at least learned that retribution is not the only consideration in sentencing, and that where retribution is appropriate, imprisonment is not the only form that retribution should take.

I think that sentencing can be looked upon in a broad sense as social work for the benefit of the public. A sentence should normally seek to mark the level of public disapproval of the offending behaviour, to deter those for whom deterrence is meaningful (not all that many, for those who are capable of being deterred have been deterred and have as a result not committed crimes in the first place) and to make unlikely the repetition of the offence by the offender. If these three aims are met, the public as a whole benefits. Since offenders differ so widely in their make-up, background, needs and abilities, however, the likelihood of repetition may vary considerably depending upon the type of sentence imposed. Imprisonment may shock one man into mending his ways: but it may also harden the anti-social attitudes of another, or finally destroy the latent good in a third. In High Court cases lengthy terms of imprisonment are often required, if only to mark the extreme disapproval of the serious criminal behaviour involved, but in the Sheriff Court, dealing as it does with much less serious criminal behaviour, imprisonment has gradually receded in importance in the interests of other disposals designed primarily to decrease the likelihood of repetition in the case of the particular offender. The art of the sentencer lies in determining where the emphasis should be placed in each case – on retribution, deterrence, or rehabilitation.

Imprisonment

'Lock them up, lock them up – that's where they should be, behind bars' is a familiar cry on the part of the public. And it may be said that Scottish and English judges have responded faithfully to this cry, since our prison population, in proportion to our total population, remains the second highest in Europe. Indeed, it has been said that the British have a penal obsession – a longing to punish, to hit back and hurt. But those who continually cry 'lock them up' often fail to realize that sometime, for better or for worse, they will have to be let out, and that (I write this with studied irony) they may not be the better for having been inside, they may even be the worse. If so, then this may mean that the wrong persons were sent to prison, or were sent for too long to prison, or that there is something wrong with the regime in prisons.

When one of my colleagues retired many years ago, he remarked to me, 'You know, sentencing's got so complicated nowadays. When I started dealing with summary crime, it was just a case of choosing between three months, sixty days or thirty days.' Three months was the normal maximum in summary criminal cases, and what my former colleague was implying was that the normal sentence was imprisonment. This would have been correct if he had been talking about the High Court, There imprisonment is to be presumed, and rightly so in many cases, for the High Court deals only with serious crime and it has to be made clear that serious crime entails the serious consequence of loss of liberty for a very long time. And prison as we know it will clearly have to remain with us for a very long time, in order to keep out of circulation those who cannot resist the temptation to wreak havoc upon the lives of their fellow men.

I sometimes think of prison as analogous to parade ground drill in the army. Mind-numbing drill is justified as being the best means so far devised for instilling a sense of discipline into recruits and maintaining a sense of discipline in trained men. Soul-destroying prison is justified as being the best means so far devised for dealing with the really serious offender. But I hope that some other means than drill will yet be devised for maintaining the army's sense of discipline. And I would like to think that other means may yet be devised for dealing with the really serious offender. A Sheriff may say 'The public must be protected', and then go on to impose a sentence of six months' imprisonment. But it would be ridiculous for him to say 'The public must be protected for six months'. If a criminal is so wicked that the public truly does require protection from him, his sentence should be imprisonment for an extended period of years, if not life. But as Sheriffs do not deal with this type of criminal, I believe that in the Sheriff Court imprisonment should be a rare occurrence.

Length of sentence

Imprisonment is an unpleasant process. Loss of liberty is bad enough. But along with that goes loss of family life, loss of dignity and loss of privacy, and, at the hands of other prisoners, exposure to bullying, drugs and sodomy. It may be necessary to accept this for long-term prisoners, but for short-term prisoners (and by definition all Sheriff Court prisoners sentenced after summary trial are short-term prisoners) the injurious effects of imprisonment on their life after release may harm rather than protect the public. There is an uncomfortable suspicion of truth about the suggestion that prison is an expensive way of making bad people worse. If, as I believe, damage is done by prison, then damage limitation may be promoted by limitation of sentence to the minimum which the circumstances may allow.

Prison regime

The old idea that people should be sent to prison *for* punishment has been replaced by the idea that people should be sent to prison *as* punishment. The very fact of being there is unpleasant enough without the further unpleasantness of such things as hard labour or bread and water diets being added. How is a prisoner to pass his time? Is it simply a question of survival? Will he be enhanced or diminished as a person by his prison service? An experienced prisoner once wrote this for me:–

Day, every day, begins for me with the clink and rattle of keys. Not a very auspicious start to a day, but normal for me, for I am a prisoner. Prisoner, convict, inmate, no matter what title is given, the stigma is there, and it is a name that will haunt me for the rest of my life. To me the most punishing part of imprisonment is when what ever sentence is given is completed the remainder of your life outside is totally dictated by the fact that you are an ex-convict. No matter whatever employment you seek to gain, the fact of the past looms between you and acceptance by a prospective employer.

The prison system I believe is calculated to humiliate and mentally destroy the person who has been sentenced. Far from being an effective deterrent, it breeds a hatred and contempt for the society that it allegedly protects. Prison is the true breeding ground of crime. I often wonder just how many crimes are planned within the confines of prison. It is easy for someone who has never broken the law to see prison as a fitting punishment, but that can only be held true in certain cases. The system as practised in this country just does not work. I believe in imprisonment, but in a manner that is practised in Scandinavia and the Netherlands. How much more effective it would be if the convicted person had an outside job to go to but in the evening had to return to the prison!

The struggle for the prison authorities is so often one of simply keeping their heads above water, for the courts show no sign of letting up on the numbers they imprison. The more insidiously the steady increase in the prison population shows itself, the less chance there is for regimes where the prisoner can be treated as an individual in his own right. This treatment, however, was at the heart of the Special Unit in Barlinnie, set up in 1973. There half a dozen of Scotland's most spectacular offenders were sent. Some particularly hard men had been in 'cages' in other prisons and had been treated more like animals than human beings; in the Special Unit they were treated as human beings unique unto themselves, and prospered accordingly. When I was first invited to the annual art exhibition in the Special Unit, I was amazed to find that no less than six of the seven inmates had been able to create paintings, sculpture and poetry of a good enough standard to merit exhibition at all. Surely, I said to myself, it cannot be the case that six out of every seven Scotsmen have such a potential? And then I remembered that to be a spectacular offender requires a high degree of creative imagination. Before they came into the Special Unit these men had never had a chance to express their creative imagination in positive and wholesome ways, and instead had channelled it into crime. But now, given the opportunity, the facilities and above all the encouragement to make the most of themselves as creators, they had become artists, and not at all bad ones at that. They had, perhaps for the first time in their lives, been shown respect as individuals, and as a result had begun to respect themselves and those with whom they lived.

My wife used to be a member of the local review committee of the parole board attached to one of our prisons. As such she once had to interview one of the Special Unit inmates. What impressed her particularly was that the man insisted on showing her around personally. He did not want the governor or a prison officer to show her round, for this was *his* thing, and his pride in what he and his fellow inmates had been able to achieve there had been very evident. If nothing else, the treatment there had gone far to promote or restore his self respect and a realization that he could do something of positive value with his life.

Alas, the Special Unit at Barlinnie is no more, but similar units (without the prefix 'Special') have been set up at both Shotts and Peterhead, with regimes which emphasise personal development, decision-making and participation in the life of the Unit as a community. Clearly, the very high level of staffing required could not possibly be sustained if such enlightened regimes were to become the norm in our prisons, but I hope that whatever regimes can be sustained in future will be designed on the fundamental Special Unit principle that prisoners are persons whose individuality and creative potential for good deserve at least as much respect as those outside.

Community service

When a crime is committed, something negative happens. The offender takes away something from his victim and thus from society – property, bodily health, or peace of mind. Imprisonment, too, is negative – society takes away the offender's liberty, privacy, family and friends. Two blacks seldom make a white, however, and while it is right that society should insist that the offender should 'pay his debt to society', there is much to be said for the idea that this payment should in appropriate cases be expressed positively rather than negatively. Hence community service. The offender does something positive to atone for the negative of his crime.

Further, imprisonment does not tend to rehabilitate. But with community service the offender may be said to be to some extent 'working out his own salvation'. Again, society benefits not only from the actual work done by the offender, but also from the increased unlikelihood of his offending again. This arises partly from the therapeutic value to the offender of work in a charitable context and partly from his being less likely to react bitterly to a society which, through its courts, has treated him not negatively as an anonymous piece of prison-fodder but positively as a person capable of doing useful work. I need scarcely add that society also benefits through not having to maintain him in prison at the cost of several hundreds of pounds per week.

Two essential features of community service orders should now be noticed. First, the work is unpaid – and so, in the interests of the trade unions, it will not be work which a man seeking paid work in the course of normal employment could expect to find. Secondly, the work is for the benefit of the community, and not for commercial concerns. Profit-making enterprises cannot expect to find a pool of free labour, nor can a private citizen expect to 'hire' an offender to work for him for nothing. Accordingly, a great deal of community service is carried out for various voluntary bodies who work for the benefit of different sections of the community. In Edinburgh some thirty such bodies have co-operated in the scheme, such as the Scotland Yard Adventure Centre, the Furniture Peg Workshop, the Craigmillar Festival Society and the Canongate Youth Project. In addition, the community service team have now established their own workshop, where skilled and semi-skilled offenders can use their abilities in projects directly organized by the team.

The Sheriff is empowered to make orders requiring the offender to carry out between 40 and 240 hours of unpaid work, the actual number chosen normally being related to the gravity of the offence. The work is to be carried out within one year. It is supervised both by the officers of the voluntary body for whom the offenders work and by a community service specialist social worker. Such a social worker will in the first instance have recommended the offender as a suitable subject for a community service order and will have chosen the type of work that he should do. Offenders may thus be found working at such diverse tasks as making furniture deliveries, driving the elderly, assisting with the handicapped, building adventure playgrounds, digging gardens, decorating houses and helping in youth clubs.

It has sometimes been suggested that community service is a 'soft option'. It is not, however, intended to be hard labour outside prison as opposed to hard labour within prison. This concept of 'hard labour' belongs to the period when the treadmill, the picking of oakum and the breaking of stones were considered to be types of labour particularly suitable for offenders. What it is intended to be is both punitive, in that considerable leisure time is confiscated, and rehabilitative – in that the offender is given the opportunity to develop an awareness of himself as a person capable of making life better, and not worse, for other people. On the matter of 'soft option', however, I might mention that some offenders have to travel some distance to reach the place where their community service work is to be done; and the question arose as to whether their travelling time should count as part of their hours of work. I am glad to say that the Edinburgh Sheriffs answered this question with a resounding 'no', taking the view that an offender could not reasonably be said to be paying any part of his debt to society by just sitting in a bus!

Community service was intended to be a direct alternative to imprisonment; Sheriffs were only supposed to make an order if they thought that a prison sentence, and not a fine, should otherwise have been imposed. This concept appeared to be rooted in the principle of making the punishment fit the crime and that imprisonment should be the normal punishment, but the more the principle of also making the punishment fit the criminal took hold, the more did Sheriffs feel inclined to make community service a sentence in its own right – i.e. without considering whether a prison sentence should otherwise have been imposed. And in my opinion, rightly so. I would go so far as to say that in cases which might otherwise merit imprisonment, community service should not be regarded as an alternative to prison, it should be the other way round – community service should be the norm, with imprisonment as an alternative.

Probation

Probation can be of great value in the right circumstances. The offender is given the opportunity of proving that he can be of good behaviour (which is normally taken to mean that he does not offend again during the period of probation), and to assist him in so doing he has the advice, guidance and friendship of a social worker. Here again I have to stress that sentencing is an art, and you can never be sure that you have done the right thing – you will never know what would have happened if you had put that man on probation instead of sending him to prison, and you will never know what would have happened if you had sent that other man to prison instead of putting him on probation. The Sheriff has to decide whether society will in the long term benefit more from a particular offender having a confidant and counsellor to steer him away from further offending than from his being locked up in the short term or fined.

Before a probation order can be made, a social enquiry report has to be obtained from the Social Work Department. On reading the social enquiry report about an offender it was often not surprising to find that he had turned to crime. Time and again you read that he had had a hopeless home life, a hopeless school life and a hopeless life without work after leaving school. No one had loved him, no one had respected him. But if a probation order is made then a new person is brought from outside into the offender's life, a social worker who has been trained to give him respect. The offender is given the confidant he may never have had before, and having a confidant must surely be a necessity in the interests of mental hygiene. He will at least be able to receive advice and guidance on such practical matters as seeking employment, obtaining social security benefits and managing a budget; he may also receive counselling, the process whereby the social worker as counsellor seeks to help the offender to find out for himself the answers to his problems. It is just possible that the offender may also be led to see the error of his ways, and having proved himself over at least the period of probation, may continue to live, if not happily ever after, then at least without troubling the courts again.

All sorts of conditions can be attached to probation orders as the Sheriff may consider appropriate for dealing with a particular offender's particular needs. There was a time, in the 1960s and 70s, when it was quite common to attach a condition of submission to psychiatric treatment, as it was believed – by psychiatrists as well as laymen – that psychiatry could assist many, if not most, offenders who were mentally less than fully fit. But a loss of confidence in psychiatry as the solution for all criminal ills appears to have set in on the part of psychiatrists. Although I continued to call for psychiatric reports when asked to do so, during the 1980s and 90s the report almost invariably concluded by saying, 'I have no psychiatric recommendation to make in this case.' But when community service is made a condition of probation, you have, I believe, an ideal type of sentence. Retribution in the form of a fine on leisure time is combined with rehabilitation in the form of advice, guidance and befriending.

One of the problems for sentencers is that they seldom hear what happens afterwards to those whom they have sentenced. You can, with some considerable effort, follow a prisoner's progress in prison but you will probably never hear how he gets on after leaving it, apart from sometimes seeing him in court yet again. When a Sheriff sees a schedule of previous convictions 'as lang's my airm', showing one prison sentence after another, there is a temptation to write the offender off as a hardened jail-bird and impose yet another prison sentence. But that situation often seemed to me to be one where probation should actively be considered. The shock of being placed on probation might just do the trick – and it was in this sort of situation that those of us who had had experience of the independent probation service particularly regretted its disappearance. For with the old-time probation officers, whom you knew and saw continually about the courts, you could follow and discuss the progress of probationers without difficulty. But latterly, all I could do – in appropriate cases – was to make it a condition of probation that the probationer and his supervising social worker came to see me in chambers, say, three or four months into the order, sometimes simply to see any progress for myself, and sometimes to give the probationer a pep-talk if the social worker was having qualms about his behaviour on probation, but was not quite sure that the order should be terminated. At any rate, it is good to know that social workers can now specialize in supervising probationers, and so a restoration of the old close relationship between Sheriffs and supervisors may become possible. One way or the other, I believe that probation is much to be encouraged.

Fines

By far the most frequently imposed sentence is the fine. Fines are purely punitive; there is nothing of rehabilitation in their use; like prison, they are negative, they take away. I suppose I first became aware of fines as a boy travelling in pre-war railway carriages. There, beside the communication cord, was a notice saying 'Penalty for improper use £5'. That gave me the idea that fines were of fixed amount. If £5 was the standard fine for this particular offence, then presumably other offences carried their own fixed fines. Later on I began to see notices warning that various types of conduct would attract a 'Maximum penalty £50'. Why, I wondered, did they never seem to say what the minimum penalty would be?

In fact there are very few fixed fines. The normal maximum in the summary criminal court is £5000 at the time of writing (it was £25 when I started as a Sheriff) and there is no such thing as a minimum fine. Within the maximum fixed by Parliament, the Sheriff has a complete discretion to fix the amount of the fine in any case. It is thus quite possible for different amounts to be fixed for the same offence by different Sheriffs, and the reason for this is not so much that Sheriffs have different views on what the amounts of fines should be as that different offenders committing the same offence do so in different circumstances, and in particular have different levels of income from which to make payment. If a fine is to have a punitive/deterrent effect, it must be set at such a level as to cause some measure of financial suffering. At the same time, humanitarian concerns dictate that the level should not be such as to cause undue financial suffering. So wide, however, is the range of income among citizens that it will at once be appreciated that what will be a severe fine for one man will be of little consequence for another. Parliament accordingly enjoined us, when fixing fines, 'to have regard to an offender's capacity to pay'.

On a visit to the courts in Sweden in 1965 I was impressed by the 'day-fine' system which was in use there. Offenders were fined so many days' income. A particular offence carried so many days' income as its fine, and detailed information as to the offender's income was readily available. All that the judge had to do was some simple arithmetic, and there he had the answer to the question of what was the appropriate fine. The system struck me as being too sophisticated to apply in Scotland, particularly as regards information about income, but the principle of it appeared to me to be wholly fair, and I happily adopted it. In their pleas-in-mitigation defence solicitors invariably informed me what their clients' weekly income was, and I accordingly thereafter and throughout my time on the Bench imposed fines related to that weekly income. I had my own rough and ready 'tariff – of one week's income for a basic breach of the peace, two weeks' for a simple theft, three weeks' for a punch-up and so on. These amounts were always starting-points, however, and were adjusted up or down according to circumstances. Thus, an unemployed youth receiving benefit of £30 per week who created a disturbance on the street was liable to a fine of about £30, while an oil worker earning £300 a week who did the same thing would be liable to a fine of around £300.

I felt that this system was both fair and reasonable, since everyone disposes of his or her whole weekly income one way or another, and thus losing a whole week's income is liable to have the same effect on all. The system had the effect of improving comparative justice, for I had long had the impression that the poor were fined too much and the rich far too little. Of course there were grumbles. For instance, I found three men to be equally guilty on the same charge; one earned £75 a week, one £180 and one £250, and I fined them £225, £540 and £750 respectively. But I pointed out to them that although the actual figures were very different, they had in fact each been fined the same, namely, three weeks' income. And there were grumbles from the rich (although they have the advantage over the poor that they can get credit when they want it), such as 'I've got my school fees to pay, I've got my golf club subscription to pay, I've got my second mortgage to pay, it soon eats up all my weekly income.' Yes, but the poor would say, 'I've got my family's food to buy, I've got my electricity to pay, I've got my baby's nappies to buy, it soon eats up my fortnightly benefit – and I can't get credit.'

I should add that I did not apply this system to road traffic cases except those involving moral weakness – drunk driving and dangerous driving. I should also add that my approach of relating fines closely to weekly income was only once tested on appeal, and I'm glad to say that the 'comparative justice' element in that approach was approved by the High Court (*Scott v Lowe* 1990 SCCR 15).

Deferred sentences

A very useful device available in Scotland is the power to defer sentence under any conditions which the Sheriff considers appropriate. That means that sentence is not imposed immediately, as it normally is, but is postponed, commonly for six months or a year, and that what the sentence will then be will depend on whether or not the offender has met the conditions on which sentence was deferred. Normally there is a general condition of good behaviour – although in practice this simply meant not coming to the notice of the police – but where appropriate, special conditions can be imposed to meet the special circumstances of the offence or offender. Before compensation orders were introduced in 1980 this was the only way to make the offender make any reparation to his victim. Sentence on a thief might be deferred, for instance, on condition that he repaid the £100 he had stolen. I would tell him that if he did make repayment he would be fined so many weeks' income, but that if he did not, he would be liable to be sent to prison. Again, before community service was introduced in 1978 this was the only way to introduce a positive or constructive element into sentencing. Sentence might be deferred, for example, in a road-rage case, on condition that the offender took the advanced driving test. The dual advantage of this approach was that while it avoided the further rage which a hefty fine might engender, it would nevertheless hit the offender's pocket – for the course of preparation for taking the test is not inexpensive. Most of all, it might help the offender to avoid raging in the future through taking pride, if he passed the test, in becoming a better and more responsible driver as a member of the Institute of Advanced Motorists.

Since I thought it was important to avoid wholly negative sentences where possible, I used this device quite a lot in my early years on the Bench. I might mention the case which for better or for worse I had to live with for years after it happened in 1968, the case of the recorder boy. A sixteen-year-old had broken into a school and had stolen a descant recorder. Why, I wondered, of all the things he might have stolen in the school had he chosen to steal a recorder? It seemed to suggest that he might even have an interest in the instrument. So I asked him if he had learnt to play the recorder at school – yes, he said, he had tried a little, but hadn't got very far. I asked him if he had a recorder now and he said he hadn't. 'All right,' I said, 'I will defer sentence for six months on condition that you buy a recorder and learn to play it to my reasonable satisfaction. If you do so, then I will only fine you £5. If you don't, then I will fine you £25.' The next thing that happened was that two or three weeks later the social work department phoned my wife and said, 'Mrs Thomson, we've got a boy here who has been told to learn to play the recorder, and you appear to be the only recorder teacher within striking distance of where he stays. Can you help?' It was indeed the case that my wife taught the recorder at that time, but it did not seem at all appropriate to either of us that she should become involved in the sentencing process, so the boy had to look elsewhere. In due course the six months passed and the day for sentencing arrived. The court was packed, with the world's press in attendance, for word had got round that a boy was to make his debut in court as a recorder player, and playing in effect for £20. Obviously it would have been ridiculous to have expected him to play in open court in such circumstances, so I retired to a side room with the fiscal and the clerk of court, and asked the press to choose just one of their number to attend. The boy showed me the recorder he said he had bought, and showed me the tutor he said he had used. I then asked him to play something. Appropriately enough, the piece he had chosen to play was 'Amazing Grace'. So he played it – but he did not play it to my reasonable satisfaction! Making every allowance for the curious circumstances in which he was playing, it did not seem to me that his heart had been in it; after six months *he should have been better than that*. However, he had gone some way to meet the conditions on which sentence had been deferred, so I compromised with a fine of £12.

This use of the power to defer sentence was much misunderstood. The conditions on which sentences were deferred were often taken to be the sentences themselves. But offenders were not sentenced to bake a cake, or help in a charity shop. They were simply being given the opportunity to do something positive and relevant to themselves or their offences with a view to reducing the negative element in their sentence. If they chose to meet the conditions, well and good, and a lighter sentence would follow. The recorder boy was not sentenced to learn the recorder, he was sentenced to pay a fine of £12. It was, if you like, a carrot and stick approach, and I always tried to spell out clearly to offenders what the sentences were likely to be if they met the conditions and what they were likely to be if they did not.

In later years people used to say to me, 'You've been very quiet lately. I haven't seen any of your funny sentences for a while.' I knew what they meant, and had to explain to them that with the arrival of community service I no longer had to think of things for people to do as special conditions of deferment of sentence – I simply made the order and the social workers who ran the community service scheme decided what the offender should do.

Essays

But the power to defer sentence remained, of course, and I still continued to use it on special conditions where it seemed appropriate. One of the special conditions which I occasionally imposed was that of writing an essay. Not surprisingly, this too was much misunderstood by the public. Awaiting sentence, I can imagine one offender saying to another, 'You'll be all right – you've got Sheriff Thomson. He'll just get you to write an essay.'

But the only situation where I would use essay-writing as a punishment was with University students appearing on charges of possessing cannabis. I felt that it was not right just to admonish them, it was absurd to send them to prison, and as students tend to have no money, it was not right to impose a fine for their parents to pay. But for a student, another essay is 'another bloody essay', and a distinct punishment at that. So I would tell them that I would admonish them on condition that they wrote, to my reasonable satisfaction, an essay of not less than 2000 words on the misuse of drugs.

Otherwise, I looked upon any essays which I occasionally gave offenders the opportunity to write as amounting to supplementary social enquiry reports. Now in passing sentence, the Sheriff can be looked upon as the chairman of a sentencing committee, the other members of the committee being the accused, his lawyer, the fiscal and, if there were background reports, the social worker, the psychiatrist and the prison governor who had written these reports. It always struck me as rather odd that two members of this committee were traditionally silent members – the fiscal and the accused. In other lands the prosecutor is a very vocal member, requesting or demanding this sentence or that. Our fiscals are far too polite to demand anything, and I would not have wished them to have done so. If the accused had gone to trial and had given evidence then I would have a reasonably good idea of what sort of person he was; but if he had pleaded guilty he would simply be a face in the dock. His lawyer would make a plea-in-mitigation, but sometimes his lawyer was too good – you felt that his client's manuscript could not possibly bear the gloss he was seeking to put upon it; again sometimes the offender's lawyer was inexperienced and you felt that he was not doing his client justice. So, after the plea-in-mitigation, it was my normal practice in common-law cases where the accused had pleaded guilty to ask him to speak for himself, by way of answering a few simple questions which I put to him from the Bench. And it was remarkable how often this gave me a better insight into the person I was dealing with, for better or for worse. Often I would call for a social enquiry report to give a still better insight, but sometimes there were cases where even after talking with the offender in court and after studying a social enquiry report I felt that there was still something missing, that I still didn't have as good a picture of the person I was dealing with as I should have. So, if he appeared to be reasonably intelligent and literate, I would defer sentence on condition that he write an essay about some feature of his life or his offending. This, as I say, was in effect by way of calling for a supplementary social enquiry report, and could be very helpful to me in trying to determine the nature of the person I was dealing with. It certainly seemed to help the offenders, who often expressed gratitude for being given the opportunity to express themselves, in their own time, about themselves. I have included a number of these essays in Appendix Two.

A National Sentencing Authority?

I have referred to sentencing being the most delicate, difficult and distasteful task for a judge to carry out. Still, the job has to be done. I would venture to make three suggestions. Firstly, the Sheriff should learn to avoid being severe for severity's sake or for the sake of the next day's headline. I think that almost all judges, from the highest to the lowest, suffer from a secret fear that *people might think they were soft*; but if in doubt, one should surely give the offender the benefit of the doubt, and err on the softer rather than the harder side. Secondly, it is always necessary to remember that each offender is a unique individual and deserves at least the respect of being treated as such. Thirdly, I agree that sentencing is sometimes too difficult a matter to be left to the judges alone. From time to time cases occur which present very difficult sentencing considerations, and in such cases I think that the Sheriff should be able to seek advice, in the same way as when dealing with children who have been prosecuted he is entitled, and in certain cases required, to seek advice from the Children's Hearing before deciding on sentence. I would like to think that a national sentencing authority could be established comparable to or absorbing the functions of the parole board, and in the same way as the parole board used to have local review committees attached to each prison, so this authority should have local committees attached to each court. The Sheriff could seek advice from such a committee where he felt he would benefit from it, but would not be obliged to accept the advice. The responsibility of passing sentence would remain his, but in selecting the sentence he would be comforted by the thought that as much as could reasonably be done to get it right had been done.

As I remarked earlier, penology is still in its infancy. It is possible that the bringing into being of a national sentencing authority could go quite some way to jolt public opinion out of its often blinkered and obsolescent thinking on the matter. It could take over the responsibility for training sentencers, for revising existing sentencing processes, for devising new methods of dealing with offenders and for introducing the monitoring of the effectiveness of all methods. In short, it could guide Cinderella's baby through the perils of infancy into the problems of childhood, and through them and beyond.

Appendix Two

Essays by Offenders

Here are extracts from a number of the essays which were written for me over the years by offenders. They were not required to write them, nor was the writing of them imposed upon them as a punishment. As I indicated in Appendix One, the offenders were simply given the opportunity of writing them as part of the sentencing process, where it seemed to me that I did not have enough information about them to make a properly informed choice of sentence, and where it also seemed to me that they were capable of writing about themselves or some aspect of the crimes in which they had been involved.

In these circumstances I would defer sentence on condition that they write an essay which I hoped would reveal something of their inner nature which had not appeared in what they or their solicitors had said in court or in what a social enquiry report had contained. In effect they were given the chance of providing a supplementary social enquiry report. In this way I hoped it would be possible to try to make the punishment fit the criminal as well as fit the crime. I should say that all the essayists gave permission for their essays to be quoted.

The demon drink

'Have a drink anytime you like – except when you feel you need one.' This was excellent advice given by Lord Kilbrandon, which I often used to quote out of court. Dealing with those who had not heard this advice or could not follow it was always difficult, and often it came down to deciding whether there was any likelihood of an offender having sufficient willpower to give it up. Sometimes an essay helped, sometimes it did not. Here is part of one of them.

I started drinking at the age of sixteen. A group of us from the office I worked in used to go for a drink at lunchtime on Fridays. This merely served to 'whet my appetite' for the evening. I remember I couldn't even eat my tea because I was so excited about going out. Even at that age I used to drink around eight to ten pints of lager on a Friday.

After I turned eighteen I progressed to drinking perhaps three or four times per week. I still ventured up town on the Friday but the start of my downfall was drinking in the traditional local pub. Soon the bar – apart from the telephone – was the only place where I could communicate with my friends and alleviate the boredom of staying in the suburbs and working in a fairly mundane office job. Soon I was finding I was in the pub perhaps six or seven nights per week. Then I sank further into the quagmire by drinking at lunchtime on days I was working and spending all day in the pubs when I wasn't. After I had got to this stage obviously something had to give.

The first consequence of my contact with alcohol was that I found that almost everytime I had been out drinking – especially on a Friday evening – I was getting involved in fights and stupid displays of aggression. Then I found I was beginning to alienate myself from the rest of my family. Although I was paid a good salary I found it wasn't enough to satisfy my very regular drinking. I soon became involved with finance companies, banks and even loan sharks. When I had exhausted all sources of raising money I turned to illegal methods, and after I had defrauded two finance companies the end came to a promising career in government service. Incredibly even all this wasn't enough to stop me from drinking heavily. Unfortunately, by this time I needed much more money than I was getting from the DHSS. Inevitably I turned to crime again and consequently found myself appearing in court to answer for my crimes. Although I am at the lowest point in my life – having been in prison – from such a low point things can surely improve.

I personally feel that the first and most important thing that I had to do to help me on the road to rehabilitation was to stand back and be honest. I understood that I had to stop deluding myself that I could take or leave alcohol. The first step that I took was to admit to a social worker that alcohol was the reason that I had committed the crimes which I have done. The social worker then referred me to a counsellor with the Royal Edinburgh.

I now see that the glamour which is associated with drinking is misplaced. Hardly an evening goes past without there being at least five advertisements for different types of drink. We are bombarded with scenes of lovely beaches, gorgeous girls and well-dressed men either with drinks in their hands or waiting in excitement for the pleasure they are going to feel after they have had a drink. There is little or no publicity about how dangerous alcohol can be. In its own way alcohol is just as dangerous, if not more, than cigarettes. Yet every packet of cigarettes has to carry a health warning and more importantly they are not allowed to advertise on television.

The personal touch

Near-alcoholics were quite often hospitalized, but as with drug addicts, any drying-out was not of much use unless the person was given the opportunity of looking inside himself with the help of a therapist, and of finding within himself the way to resolve whatever problems had led to his addiction. If a man claimed he was 'coming off the drink' I would sometimes invite him to write about it so that I could form a better view of his intentions.

Due to my indulgence I have lost two partners whom I cared for very much, three jobs, my accommodation, the respect of my family and my self-respect – the list is endless! During my four weeks in hospital, my mind was in a state of torment. I kept asking myself questions like Why am I so pathetic? Why do I suffer from this horrible problem? What caused it? Did anything cause it? I honestly thought I'd ruined my life, but I was given hope and encouragement. I fought back and was really determined to beat my problem. However, regrettably I failed and relapsed. The disappointment and bewilderment that one feels when this happens is almost unbearable.

Although I'd been admitted to hospital because of this problem, and had treatment accordingly, I never really found the hospital beneficial. But thank God that since I've started my programme with the Edinburgh Council on Alcoholism I'm coping better than I ever imagined. With my counsellor it is totally different. It is on a one-to-one basis and I can speak about aspects of my life that would normally inhibit me in front of a group of people, which is what the norm was in hospital. The regular meetings with my counsellor are, I find, very intimate, and sometimes stressful. But I do find them helpful and to a certain extent successful. I say 'to a certain extent' because at the moment I still find coping without my daily intake quite hard, but I'm managing – just! But I am managing and that's all that really matters to me.

Although this is probably the most difficult task I've tackled, at least I'm coping. I take one day at a time, and 'throw myself' into work. I keep my regular appointments with my counsellor because I know I have to. And they help.

Hell on earth

When prisoners were brought up from the cells into court I often tried to guess what the charge against them would be, just by seeing what they looked like. I usually got it wrong, for appearances are deceptive, but there was normally no difficulty with those on drugs charges – so often did they have a worn and weary zombie-like appearance. One young woman did not seem to fit in to the usual pattern, however, being well-spoken, presentable and intelligent, and I wasn't sure if she really had been fully into the drugs scene in which she was alleged to have been. Her essay, alas, removed the doubt.

It all started with a few joints of hash. And then one day I asked Jean if she would get me a fix of smack. I was dying to try it. If I'd known then what I know now I would have run straight back to life and never come back.

I never got hooked for the first three years. I just used to fix maybe once every two or three weeks. And then all of a sudden things started to go wrong. I lost my job, broke off my engagement, the next thing I knew I was fixing more and more. That's when I started shoplifting and various other crimes. It was like a nightmare. I went from being an average female into being a drug-crazed monster. I didn't stop to think what I was doing to my family and friends. I convinced myself I knew what I was doing. But you don't know with drugs – that's all you live for, you make money to get drugs and more money and more drugs. Nobody would lend me any because they didn't trust me anymore. I was at my wit's end when I met a friend who said, 'Well about your only option now is to go down the shore.'

I nearly died. Prostitution was the last thing I had imagined. I just stood looking at her. She said, 'Well?' I said, 'Oh I don't know – I couldn't – My man Carl would kill me! She said he'd never find out if it was just the once. So I said OK. It was all over in about an hour and I had £50. I rushed up and bought me and Carl a fix. I felt awful, really cheap. When Carl asked where I'd got so much money I said I'd stolen it and he believed me. I never went back at first and then I was stuck again one night. So off I went again. This time I met Carl's sister-in-law as she was at it as well. I left Carl soon after that.

I got heavier and heavier into drugs. I was taking everything. I was using £100 worth of drugs a day. So as you can imagine I was walking the streets soliciting every night. Soon I was selling drugs and moved in with the guy who was supplying nearly three-quarters of Edinburgh with drugs. The money that was involved was unreal. Sometimes I had to count it out. One time it amounted to £70,000. I had never seen so much money. My habit had got worse. I was using nearly £200–300 worth a day.

I suppose the guy I was living with was a drugs baron. Anyway he got caught eventually and got eight years. So I was back on the streets again. Then Carl came back, having been in jail himself, but after only two months out he was found dead in a stair, the needle still in his arm. Drugs kill people and destroy and tear apart families. You've no friends when you are a junkie, because nobody trusts you. It's a very cold and lonely existence. A junkie would do anything for a fix because sometimes the pain is unbearable. I've been to hell and I didn't die to do it cause you can make your own hell on earth by starting to inject. I don't know if I'll ever inject again because you can never tell if you'll fall by the wayside, but I don't want to die of an overdose or Aids. I want to see my baby grow up. I think if she ever got involved I would just die.

Taxi!

It was very seldom that anyone ever admitted in court to being a drug addict. Normally everyone had given it up last year or at the end of last month or at the beginning of this week. One of them was even more than usually unconvincing in his protestations, so I gave him the opportunity of writing an essay on 'The escape from heroin'. What he wrote avoided the subject completely, but nevertheless gave an unexpected insight into a day in the life of an addict.

Thank God I am now free from heroin and no longer have to regard myself a junkie. But when I was hopelessly addicted I had to get at

*least £100 worth of smack a day to satisfy my craving. My only means
of raising this sort of money was by theft, and that meant breaking
into people's houses and stealing the most easily taken things, usually
the video recorder. The reason for this was that video recorders used
to cost about £500 in the shops, and you could usually expect to find
someone in a pub who would buy one from you for £100. My day
revolved round a taxi. I would start the day by phoning for a taxi
which would take me to the part of Edinburgh where I had decided
to carry out my housebreakings for the day. The taxi would drop me
off, but I would tell the driver not to go away in case I wasn't able
to break in to the houses I had tried in that part of the town. And if
there was nothing doing, I would get him to take me to the next part
of Edinburgh on my list. Then when eventually I got my video for
the day, the taxi was standing by waiting to take me off to the pub
to try to flog it there. There might not be any punter there who was
interested, so I got back into the taxi – sometimes they just kept their
engines running – and went off to the next pub where I hoped I could
do business. It might take one or two more taxi rides till I eventually
got the video sold. After that of course I had to get to my dealer to get
my fix, so back into the taxi. And if my dealer was out of gear for the
day then I'd get the driver to take me to the next dealer and the next
again until at last I got what I needed. For me for a time life would
have been unthinkable without heroin and without taxis.*

The Eskimo artist

A sixteen-year-old boy was convicted by a jury of reckless fire-
raising. He had defended himself, however, and had done so
with such ability that because of this, and because a social enquiry
report did not seem to me to 'have got inside him', I wanted to
hear what he had to say himself about what he was like. As a result
of his essay I realized I was dealing with an even more unusual boy
than I had at first thought; and so I put him on probation with
a condition that he attend classes in creative writing. This is part
of what he wrote for me at sixteen:–

*On writing this essay I must express my amusement at the speculation
which has surrounded the whole thing before I even wrote it, ever
since the news came out that I had to write one. The number of people
(mostly my own age) who have offered to write or tell me what to*

write has been quite extraordinary. It seems that everyone has been waiting on a chance like this to tell you something, especially the younger ones.

I think the root of my trouble was in school. At about the age of eleven I was already destined (according to the staff) to become a delinquent and they more or less just left me to my own fate which, I suppose, was not too bad because they stopped trying to force-feed me with their morals and principles and I grew up learning about them myself. I believe they should do that with every child instead of trying to make them replicas of themselves. Eskimo artists when carving ivory do not begin by deciding what to carve, they say 'I wonder what is inside' and as they carve they gradually find it, it was there waiting for discovery and release.

I feel it is essential to hold an opinion on everything as to remain indifferent is a mortal sin. The true opposite of love is not hate but indifference. Hate, bad as it is, at least treats the neighbour as a he or she, whereas indifference turns the neighbour into an it or a thing. That is why there is actually one thing worse than evil and that is indifference to evil. In human relations the nadir of morality, the lowest point as far as Christian ethics is concerned, is manifest in the phrase 'I couldn't care less' and too many people couldn't.

Thank you, Sir, for letting me try and express myself, although I doubt if you will be able to understand me any better from this confusing essay. I think Oscar Wilde summed it up rather nicely when he said 'The criminal classes are as near to us that even the policeman can see them, they are so far away from us that only the poet can understand them.'

Thereafter, from time to time over the years, he sent me examples of his literary work, which eventually found publication in a literary periodical.

Prison doesn't work

A man was charged on indictment with stealing a bottle of whisky and some £3 in cash. The fact that he had been placed on indictment indicated that the fiscal expected a sentence of at least six months' imprisonment. His record showed that he had been sent to prison on each of the previous four occasions he had appeared before the courts, and this no doubt weighed with the fiscal in placing him on indictment. I was astonished, however, that the fiscal expected such a sentence for theft of such a small amount. The man appeared to be intelligent, and I took the view that the shock of being placed on probation might bring about a change in his life that prison had not done. So I deferred sentence on condition that he wrote an essay about the effect of imprisonment on him. He wrote this in 1972:–

You have set me a difficult task in writing this essay as never before have I really given the matter any serious thought.

My first venture into crime was in 1944 when I was eight years old. My parents were good people and at times went without things themselves to give to myself and two older brothers. My father was seriously injured in a mining accident and spent years in and out of hospital. I became jealous of my friends getting things we could not afford. Led by an older boy I turned to theft to try and get them. I think it is a form of escapism with me now, as whenever I am depressed or under any great pressure I seem to commit a stupid offence, get caught and sent to prison. I say stupid as I never show any profit from any of my crimes.

Prison is a completely different world from the normal one. It is a breeding ground for crime, and the only topic of conversation between prisoners is crime, past and in the future. Nothing is ever done to rehabilitate anyone unfortunate enough to find themselves here. If you seek assistance you are classified as a nuisance or a trouble-maker. A prisoner preferring his own company is said to be anti-social, the company of one other prisoner, he is said to be homosexual, more than one he is part of gang. Therefore in this world of losers he continues to be a loser. He is locked in a cell with two other prisoners that was originally built for one. This cell is his living room, bedroom, dining room and toilet. It means living like an animal and at times feeling like one, thus destroying his self-respect. The prison staff seem to feel that the more they can keep you in the cell the easier their job is.

On release from prison a prisoner who has served over three months is given a grant of £4 [£49.50 at the time of writing]. This has to keep him for a week, even if he has a family to support. This means a struggle right from the start, and the fact that he has a criminal record makes it difficult for him to attain employment. I don't want to create the impression that I have a persecution complex. I know now that I have been my own worst enemy and society had to be protected.

Through writing this I have had to think and I now realize that the ones who really pay for my stupidity are my children, through being deprived of my earnings and the torment they get at school by not having a proper uniform and being taunted about their father being a jail-bird.

This struck me as being a forceful indictment of prison as a useless institution, and I had no hesitation in making a probation order. I enquired about him five years later, and was glad to find that he had been in no further trouble.

This sporting life

A man was charged – along with two girls – with committing a breach of the peace through taking part in a piece of anti-hunt sabotage. The man's involvement appeared to have consisted in agreeing to take the two girls, who were card-carrying saboteurs, to the scene of the planned sabotage. Such was the evidence that I had to find them all guilty, but I had considerable doubt as to whether the man was a genuine saboteur. I accordingly deferred sentence on condition that he write an essay on the morality of hunting and fishing.

'Sport may be defined as the fair, difficult, exciting, perhaps dangerous, pursuit of a wild animal, who has the odds in his favour, whose courage, strength, speed or cunning are more or less a match for or superior to our own, whose natural instinct engages a considerable amount of our intelligence to overcome it and whose death, being of service, is justifiable.'

So wrote Lord Walsingham, a prominent Victorian author who wrote on all aspects of fishing and shooting. How well has his definition of the morality of bloodsports stood the test of time (if, indeed, morality has a temporal dimension) and what relevance has it to the issue in question?

Perhaps the first point of controversy would be contained in the terms 'fair' and 'odds in his favour'. On a purely statistical basis there is a clear distinction between fox-hunting and angling. Sixty mounted riders, thirty pairs of hounds, terrier dogs, professional full-time huntsmen and a clutch of hired hands versus 'the fox' does seem to smack a trifle of overkill. If one adds to this the apparently verifiable cases in which foxes have been kept in artificial lairs with the stated purpose of 'keeping foxes alive to hunt' then one must certainly question the modern-day version of Lord Walsingham's 'Queensberry Rules'.

The fish, on the other hand, is most unlikely to be caught in the average river. Unlike the fox, he is not chased out of his natural habitat nor is he a minority in the ratio of hunter to hunted. Hunted he may be, persecuted he is not.

To anyone who has observed both sports a clear distinction is evident in the amount of intelligence required. To the average fox-hunt the initial intelligent organization is at a maximum prior to the commencement of the hunt and then rapidly diminishes during its course with hounds being split up and lost and the field fragmenting as the day goes on. On the other hand, the average angler selects his area carefully based on a combination of many factors such as wind, tide, sun conditions and past experience not to mention the wide range of options open to him in terms of selection of equipment. Thereafter he may be called upon for many hours to exhibit the quality of patience. Even after his luring tactics have been successful the contest is not over. Single-handedly he must land his victim against opposition not only from the fish but also from such factors as line-breaking strain and snags on rocks and debris.

The poor fox has no such allies after he has been cornered. If he is not forced out of his cul-de-sac by terriers he can but wait for the inevitable as he is dug out of his earth by men wielding spades to meet his death at the centre of a closed circles of dogs and hunters. If he's lucky his despatch is via a single pistol shot – more likely he will endure the agony of a permitted disembowelling by numerous dogs.

But, of course, the area in which the largest void exists between fox-hunting and angling is succinctly captured in Walsingham's phrase – 'whose death, being of service, is justifiable'. There is a direct contrast here because, quite simply, angling often does not result in death. The competitive fisherman is interested in the skill of the pursuit and in its results in terms of gross poundage for comparative purposes. Then he returns his quarry to its native environment – alive! In the fox-hunt the kill is the high point of the day's events. Dejection and demoralization (as well as dwindling numbers) are apparent if a fox-hunt has not killed over successive outings.

Even if the fish is taken from the water it can be argued to the satisfaction of any intelligent person that its death is of service (whether that service is necessary is quite a different matter). At least the fish makes a contribution to the diet of another species whereas no gastronomic delights such as 'fox's legs', 'brush soup' or 'rice Reynard' are known to exist.

It may be argued that the countryside is being rid of a predatory pest in the case of a fox, who, if left alone, would multiply in a fashion normally attributed to the much-suffering rabbit. One wonders, then, why this threatened population explosion has not yet taken place. Why, in the 1980s, is Twentieth Century Fox better known as a failed film company rather than as a breed likely to inherit the earth? Or, in the case of foxes, earths. Is it not more likely that the fox, as a species, exists under exactly the same conditions as the rest of us do? i.e. its growth rate is determined by its available food supply within its daily search area.

Using the fox-hunters' own figures the total fox population in the UK is reckoned to be around 900,000 animals. Of this figure 30,000 are killed each year by various means, including 9,000 by fox-hunts. In other words, fox-hunting accounts for about a 1% reduction in the population each year – a figure quite insignificant when compared with the number of deaths from natural causes. In any event, a more expensive and less efficient method of population control would be hard to imagine. So the concept of a service-giving death is quite indefensible in the case of fox-hunting.

But so far we have concentrated only on a Victorian definition of the morality of hunting. Whilst such matters may have seemed eminently clear to the mind of Lord Walsingham, time, civilisation and science have thrown new light on these affairs. He never attempted to deal with the concept of the 'sentient being' – a being which feels stress, panic and impending death in an emotional as well as physiological sense.

Not too many years ago this might have been yet another area of difference between the hunt of a warm-blooded fox and a cold-blooded fish. The physiological signs of being hunted would be much more obvious in the case of the fox. But recent studies (Peters, Institute of Hydro-Biology, University of Hamburg) have established clear signs of stress in fish comparable to that of other vertebrates, including mammals. The fact that we cannot hear a fish scream in pain should give us no cause for comfort. What illogical mental computer allows us to be revolted when a fox is ripped to death but to accept the suffocation of a fish without question?

As we grow slowly wiser and, paradoxically, slowly humbler in the ways of the Universe there must surely come a time at which we have the confidence to set ourselves free from the comforting support of past practices. We don't need to kill the fish to live any more than we need to kill the fox. Can the fact that it's a slightly more distant species have something to do with it? Is it not really the fact that it's our own minds which are unable to bridge the divide to more distant species? It seems apparent that our inability to tolerate cruelty to different species is inversely proportional to how likely they are to sit on our knee. And as a moral basis for taking life that leaves a lot to be desired.

Our own moral guidelines in this country have always been influenced by the flexible and responsive attitudes of the established churches; perhaps too flexible and too responsive to the wrong people. There are exceptions. St Francis of Assisi for one. 'Not to hurt our humble brethren is our first duty to them, but to stop there is not enough. We have a higher mission – to be of service to them whenever they require it.' That statement certainly doesn't allow for any exceptions.

I did not think that a real anti-hunt saboteur could possibly have written such an intelligent and witty essay, and I accordingly admonished him.

Index